DIAMOND HEART

Book Three

Being and the Meaning of Life

DIAMOND HEART

Book Three

Being and
the Meaning of Life

A. H. Almaas

Diamond Books  Berkeley, California

Cover photo: © section from "Shrine on Mt. Tateyama, Japan" by Galen Rowell/ Mountain Light, 1988; opening quote from *The World As I See It,* Albert Einstein, Citadel Press, 1979.

First published in 1990 by

Diamond Books
Almaas Publications
P.O. Box 10114
Berkeley, CA 94709

Second Printing / November 1994

ISBN 0-936713-05-4

Library of Congress Card Catalog Number: 90–081060

Typeset in 11 point Galliard Roman by Byron Brown
on a Macintosh computer, using QuarkXpress
& output on a Linotronic 300

Printed in the United States by Thomson-Shore
on recycled paper

It is very difficult to explain this feeling to anyone who is entirely without it, especially as there is no anthropomorphic conception of God corresponding to it. The individual feels the nothingness of human desires and aims and the sublimity and marvelous order which reveal themselves both in nature and in the world of thought. He looks upon individual experience as a sort of prison and wants to experience the universe as a single significant whole.

— Albert Einstein
from *The World As I See It*

TABLE OF CONTENTS

PREFACE

We live in a world of mystery, wonder, and beauty. But most of us seldom participate in this real world, being aware rather of a world that is mostly strife, suffering, or meaninglessness. This situation is basically due to our not realizing and living our full human potential. This potential can be actualized by the realization and development of the human Essence. The human Essence is the part of us that is innate and real, and which can participate in the real world.

This series of books, **Diamond Heart**, is a transcription of talks I have given to inner work groups in both California and Colorado, for several years, as part of the work of these groups. The purpose of the talks is to guide and orient individuals who are intensely engaged in doing the difficult work of essential realization.

The talks are organized in a manner that shows the various states and stages of realization in the order that occurs for the typical student, at least in our teaching method: the Diamond Approach. They begin with the states, knowledge, and questions most needed for starting the work on oneself, proceeding to stages of increasing depth and subtlety, and culminating in detailed understanding of the most mature states and conditions of realization.

Each talk elucidates a certain state of Essence or Being. The relevant psychological issues and barriers are discussed precisely and specifically, using modern psychological understanding in relation to the state of Being, and in relation to one's mind, life and process of inner unfoldment.

Hence, this series is not only a detailed and specific guidance for the student, but also an expression and manifestation of the unfoldment of the human Essence as it reveals the mystery, wonder, exquisiteness, and richness of the real world, our true inheritance. Each talk is actually the expression of a certain aspect or dimension of Being as it descends into the consciousness of the teacher in response to the present needs of the students. The teacher acts both as an embodiment of such reality and as a channel for the living knowledge that is part of this embodiment.

It is my wish that more of my fellow human beings participate in our real world, and taste the incredible beauty and integrity of being a human being, a full manifestation of the love of the truth.

Richmond, California 1986

INTRODUCTION
to Book Three

The process of essential self-realization goes through several stages, each with associated essential states, psychological issues, and resulting wisdom. The conceptualization of these stages depends partly on the teaching one is following, and partly on the focus of study. In the Diamond Approach the teaching is oriented towards the natural and spontaneous revelation of the truth of the Soul as one investigates one's experience, motivated by the pure love for truth and joy in it.

The first naturally occurring stage is that of the discovery of Essence, which is the true nature of the Soul. Essence is discovered directly in experience as a fundamental presence that manifests in many qualities that we call aspects. It is recognized for what it is, and understood as the true resolution for the various existential deficiencies and longings of the ego and its personality. The second stage becomes the objective understanding of the ego and the mind, now using the wisdom available from the presence of Essence. The contrast to Essence provides the mirror in which the personality of ego becomes understood in a precise and clear way.

This then makes it possible to move to the third stage, where one's sense of identity shifts from ego to Essence. The first book of this series focused on the first stage, and the second book on the second. The present book is concerned mostly with the third stage, that of self-realization proper. The issues here are not the various deficiencies, conflicts, and longings of the personality, but those of self and identity. It is a matter of seeing that although Essence is discovered and understood for what it is, there is still identification with ego. At this stage one is dealing with the issue of being an entity experiencing Essence, rather than finding it to be one's very self and identity.

This shift of identity shifts one's center from ego to Essence, making the presence of Essence the center of one's universe of experience. This confronts and dissolves deeply rooted, and hitherto unquestioned, ego structures. One's view of oneself and the universe undergoes a fundamental transformation. Many things that have been taken till this point to be fundamental facts of reality are seen here to be only beliefs and naive assumptions.

This also leads to objectivity about Essence itself, for now it is experienced from its own vantage point, rather than from that of the personality. Essence is recognized as Being, time-lessness, the eternal now. The book discusses the state of self-realization on both the individual and universal dimensions—the first, centered around timelessness, functions as the entry to the latter, which is centered around the nowness of the oneness of Being.

The actual experiences, realizations, insights, and the resulting wisdom, are elaborated in specific detail, and the corresponding ego issues and structures are clarified enough so they can be seen in oneself. The states and issues discussed are of an advanced nature, and the reader needs to relate them to his/her intimate experience to avoid degenerating the material into mere intellectual knowledge. The intention of these books is to be of practical benefit to the reader. In order to metabolize the true nourishment that can be gained from the explorations in this book, the reader needs to participate fully, by looking at his/her experience with the kind of sincerity required from any real student of the Work.

DIAMOND HEART
Book Three
Being and the Meaning of Life

ONE

The Flame of the Search

Why am I here? Where am I going? We need to see how honest we can be with ourselves when trying to answer these questions. These two questions are related; that is, most people think they are here because there is a goal, they want to go somewhere. Where do you want to go? You probably think you know; do you? Do you think I know where you should go? If you think I know, can I tell you? And if I tell you, will you follow? Can you follow?

These are questions that you cannot answer with your mind. These are questions that should remain questions. Do not try to simply answer them mentally. These questions are like a flame. If you answer them with your mind, you will put out the flame, because the mind doesn't, the mind can't

1

know the answers to these questions. When you answer them with your mind and you think you know, the question is gone. When you believe you have answered such questions, the flame is gone and there is no more inquiry.

If you settle for answers on this level, you will live like most of humanity, who assume that they know why they are here and where they are going. Such a life typically feels shallow and insignificant. A life with no fundamental questioning is a life lived according to formulas, according to what one has heard from others. But why should you believe what others tell you about life? You don't actually know yet what is true for you, what is important for you, what will work for you.

It is better to remain ignorant than to pretend knowledge. If you know that you are ignorant and don't pretend otherwise, there is a question that stays alive and continues to burn in you, a deep hunger for the truth.

If you look at every moment of your life, such as this moment, you will see that most of the time you believe that you know what is the best thing for you at that moment. You think, feel, and behave as if you know what is supposed to happen, as if you know what you want and what is important to want. You live your life believing at every moment that you know how you should be. Where does this knowledge come from?

Most of it comes from your early childhood, both from what you were directly taught and by what you indirectly absorbed from your surroundings. Some of it comes from what you have heard or read. It is conditioned knowledge. Whatever the source, conditioned knowledge is useless in answering the fundamental questions, such as the question of why we are here. The conditioned knowledge says that what I'm here for is to be happy, to be successful, to feel good, to get what I think I want, to satisfy my dreams, to get someone to love me, or to make a lot of money. The conditioning is simply a mechanism for survival. You have survived, you are here—so that knowledge has done, and is doing, its job. If you want to continue merely surviving, you can. But what difference is there then between you and any animal, any insect that is born, lives and dies?

So the conditioned knowledge says that what I'm here for is to be happy, to be successful, to feel good, to get what I think I want, to satisfy my dreams, to get somebody to love me, or to make a lot of money. This is the knowledge that you have been conditioned with, and it is useless for answering fundamental questions.

How do you know that the knowledge you get from others is the truth? How do you know that your teachers, or even the great philosophers, have the answer that is appropriate for you? Christ says to love your neighbor. Do you really know that that is what you need to do? Buddha says that enlightenment is the best thing. How do you know that is what you need?

Some people say you have to learn to be yourself. It sounds good. Some people say you should be free from your personality and develop your Essence. It sounds great. How do you know it will resolve your situation? You don't really know whether any of these ideas are relevant or true for you. You can't know with certainty until you have experimented and learned from your own experience. Until then your action is based on faith or belief. If you assume unquestioningly that what someone else says is the truth, your inner flame will be extinguished. You will believe that you have answered questions when you haven't answered them; someone else has. And they haven't answered them for you, but for themselves. We comfort ourselves by believing that others know, and that we can use their knowledge. It's a very comforting thought; it encourages us to be lazy. We comfort ourselves by saying to ourselves, "Somebody knows, and in time I'll get around to studying it. It's already known and always available to me."

But do you, yourself, really know in your heart what is supposed to happen? Do you ever allow yourself to question, to have a burning question—and not put out the flame quickly with the first answer that you hear? You put out the flame so that you can return to your sense of comfort and security.

Someone tells you that it's good to pay attention, to be aware. When you try it, it helps a little—but you still don't know whether it's the answer. You don't know whether it will actually resolve your situation. And if you believe you know, you're lying to yourself. You need to keep the question alive while you investigate for yourself.

Our questions about why we are here and where we are going are uncomfortable, but they are real questions for every human being. If you do not ask them, and allow them to be ongoing questions, you will never know for yourself what it's all about. You will never know who you are, why you're here, and where you are going. Your mind is full of ideas and dreams and plans about what will fulfill you, what will make you happy, what will give you freedom. But these ideas silence the question, comfort your mind, and put out the flame.

So begin with the awareness that you don't know the answers. And be aware of the feverish attempts in your mind to convince yourself that you know. It's not only that you don't know the answers, you don't know whether the questions can be answered. Can you allow the questions to remain if you don't know whether there is an answer? Can you be that sincere with yourself? You believe you're here because you believe you can get something here, you believe you can experience something here, you hope you can find some freedom here. But do you really know that? Are you certain that what we are doing is right for you? Can you ever be certain if you don't answer the questions for yourself?

Perhaps you have heard the idea that if you think you need love, you need to love others, be selfless. It sounds good.

It's what the great masters say. But for you it is hearsay, a rumor, a possibility worth inquiring about. It is not knowledge yet. Is it possible to leave your ideas, your thoughts, your knowledge behind, and let the inquiry be? Can you let the question stand? Can you for a while forget all your formulas, all of what you have heard or read, everything your parents said or didn't say, what all the great teachers have said, and remain alone with the question? Why are you here? Where are you going? What is it all about? Can you let yourself have that question intensely—can you let that flame burn in you without needing to put it out with an answer?

Can we let this inquiry deepen in us, in our hearts, in our bellies, in our being? Can we let our being be a question mark, a yearning? It is a motiveless search, a search that does not depend on any ideas about going somewhere. There is no goal in sight, so it becomes a flame that continues to burn and deepen with time. Don't cover it up, put it out, or let it go; just let it be. Let it consume you. Let it burn away all your ideas and beliefs about how things should be. Let it burn away all your concepts about good and bad. Let that inquiry deepen and expand, so that you can forget. Let go of all you have learned ... for a while at least.

Can you exist as an inquiry, an inquiry into the truth? Are you here just to live, work, eat, love, hate, have children, and die? Can you let go of what you believe you have? Can your mind empty itself of all your possessions, beliefs, theories, knowledge, understanding, and simply remain as a search, a pure inquiry not influenced by anyone or anything, even your own past? Even if you felt love and freedom and relaxation and so on in the past, what makes you think these things are what you need at this moment? The insights you had in the past might have been right, but how do you know they are what you need now and in the future? In order to find out, all you can do is let them go. Can you remain completely ignorant, unknowing; can you let your mind go, not impose anything on your mind, and at the same time not go dead, not become unconscious?

Can we rid ourselves of all influences, of the influences of others' ideas and of our own past, and remain in the now, as an inquiry? You can observe that every time someone says something that sounds true, or every time you have an insight, you say, "Oh, wonderful, that must be it." You want to put out the flame. You want the first answer that comes to silence the questioning.

Why are we in such haste to have answers? We jump on the first promise of salvation that comes. Why not stay with the question? What makes you think that salvation is the answer, that freedom is the answer? What makes you think that enlightenment is the answer? What makes you think that love is the answer? You might feel that you want these things, but how do you know that getting them is the best thing that could happen in this moment? How do you know whether you're supposed to be dead or alive, rich or poor, free or enslaved? Is it possible to let your mind be free?

I am not trying to give you an answer; I'm just giving you a question. You need to let your being be ablaze like a flame, an aspiring flame, with no preconceived ideas about what it aspires to. To be just burning intensely, deeply wanting to know, wanting to see the truth without following any pre-conceptions, totally in the present with the question itself, and let it burn away all the ideas, all the beliefs, all the concepts, even the ones you learned from the great teachings. If you don't allow that flame completely, will you ever rest in your life? Will you ever rest in your life as long as you're covering up your question, answering it before it's really answered? Will you ever really be content with someone else's answer?

As you see, it is a completely personal quest. It is your situation, your life, your mind; no one else can answer these questions for you. Whatever answer comes from outside, belongs to the outside; you can try it on for size, but you must make your own inquiry. You can explore any suggestion, any guidance, but you need to keep the inquiry going. Don't just silence it because you have heard something that sounds right. Without this sincere questioning, this motiveless search—without this flame—the Work cannot be done. Without the flame, any work is done simply according to ideas and beliefs.

The Work must be done according to your own inquiry; the Work that we do here is only a guidance. Your motivation has to be pure, real and true; your flame has to be there; otherwise you'll use the Work for the wrong purpose. You'll get somewhere according to an idea, but it is not necessarily where your Being would take you without constraint. You can develop this and that, become free from this and that, but how do you know whether that will fulfill your destiny? You might think you're supposed to be more loving, or less afraid, or more comfortable, or more relaxed, or richer, or more beautiful. Maybe you are, maybe not. These are just ideas. But true questioning, sincere questioning doesn't have a particular goal. If you think you have a goal, an end, and if you think you're going to go there, you've already extinguished the flame. If you've told yourself you're here because you want to be enlightened, you want to be free, you want to be loving, you want to be this or that, that means that you already know.

But you don't know, really. It's a lie to believe that you know. It's true that there's a question and that you don't know the answer—that is the truth. The most honest answer you can give to the question "Why am I here?" is that I am here because I don't know. The truest reason for you to be here is to fan that flame of inquiry.

These questions are not theoretical or philosophical. They are at the root and heart of your life, relevant for every moment of your life, whatever you're doing. If you don't know but you're pretending that you know, you're wasting the moment. It's a complete waste, regardless of what you're doing. It's not only that the idea in your mind might be the wrong one for you—the fact that it is an idea, instead of a direct perception, puts out the flame of the search, and your unfoldment is blocked. Whenever the answer is not a direct perception it will block or distort your experience.

What I'm saying is not meant to lead you to blame yourself for believing that you know. It's not a matter of trying to make you "good." No, we're trying to see the truth. You need to see clearly all the ways that you snuff out the flame, and how consistently you silence the question.

You might do some work on yourself and have a wonderful experience, a great insight or state. But how do you know that this wonderful experience is what is needed right now? How do you know that the knowledge you think you're getting will resolve your situation? The flame must continue. The fire of inquiry needs to be fed, needs to grow, to intensify, to deepen. Our inquiry needs to be directed not at trying to reduce it, but to letting it grow. The flame needs to burn away all the rest, to grow until it answers itself by itself becoming the fulfillment. The fire of that inquiry can burn away all the dross, all the resistance, all the ideas, all the accumulation of the past so you can actually see what is really there, the whole picture in the present moment without needing to depend on anything from the past or on anyone else's experience. When you know in the moment without any influence, then you can completely be alone with your own truth. Without that, it's obvious that you can't know with certainty. Only with that certainty can life become significant. If you know, for yourself, who you are, you will know where you are going, and you will be fulfilled.

Yes, there are guidance and help here, but not to give answers, only to help you inquire. This Work is to encourage your own inner development, whatever that may be, to help you remain alone with your inquiry. It can be difficult to be alone with yourself. We are not usually supported or encouraged to let our being just be, to be authentic, and not an imitation or a reaction. You can be open, listening to what others suggest, but these things are only possibilities; you still need to inquire by yourself within the intimacy of your own heart. Is this answer your own experience, your answer? You need to be completely open, and not use what you hear to comfort yourself. You need to use it to add fuel to your inquiry.

Can you let yourself be completely intimate with yourself, completely uninfluenced and unbiased? Can you let this inquiry, this flame, burn in the intimacy, in the utter aloneness within?

TWO

Are You Here?

Some weeks ago we asked, "Why are you here?" Now we will get down to an even more fundamental question: "Are you here?" Are you really here in this room? I don't mean is your body here, because that is obviously the case. But are *you* here? Do you feel that you are here in the room? Are you aware of being present here, and of your actual experience in this moment? Or are you lost in thoughts, fantasies, plans, emotional reactions? Are you here, or are you busy liking and disliking? Are you here, or are you busy judging yourself and everything else?

Are you here now, or are you trying to be here, making a token effort because this is what we are talking about? Are you aware of everything and everyone around you? Are you aware of your surroundings, or are you lost in a whirlwind of thoughts? When you hear the question, "Are you here?" it's not important in answering that you try to be good or correct. It's important only to sincerely explore for yourself, are you here or not? Are you in your body or oblivious, or only aware of parts of it? When I say, "Are you in your body?" I mean, "Are you completely filling your body?" I want to know whether you are in your feet, or just have feet. Do you live in them, or are they just things you use when you walk? Are you in your belly, or do you just know vaguely that you have a belly? Or is it just for food?

Are you really in your hands, or do you move them from a distance? Are you present in your cells, inhabiting and filling your body? If you aren't in your body, what significance is there in your experience this moment? Are you preparing, so that you can be here in the future? Are you setting up conditions by saying to yourself, "When such and such happens I'll have time, I'll be here"? If you are not here, what are you saving yourself for?

Regardless of the stories you tell yourself, at this moment, this very moment, there is only this moment, here, now. Nothing else exists. For your direct experience, only the here and now is relevant. Only now is real. And it is always like that. At each moment, only that moment exists. So we need to ask why we put ourselves on hold, waiting for the right time, waiting for the right circumstances to arise in the future. Maybe the right time will never come. Maybe the conditions you have in mind will never come together for you. When will you begin to exist then? When will you begin to be here, to live? Regardless of the ideas about past and future that dominate your experience, right at this moment only this moment exists, and only this moment has any significance for you. The most direct and obvious fact of experience is that the moment, the here and now, is all that exists. This is all there is for this moment. Whatever is happening at this moment, that is your life. The future is not your life; it never arrives. What is actually here is always only this moment.

So can you let yourself be? I am not suggesting that you let yourself be to get anything or do anything, even to understand anything. I mean just to be. Are you giving yourself the simple privilege of being, of existence? Why do you think that what you do, what you have, what you get or don't get are more important than just being here? Why are you always wanting to get something or go somewhere? Why not just relax and be here, simply existing in all your cells, inhabiting all your body? When are you going to let yourself descend from your lofty preoccupations, and simply land where you are?

Stop striving after all kinds of things; stop dreaming, scheming, planning, working, achieving, attempting, moving, manipulating, trying to be something, trying to get somewhere. You forget the simplest, most obvious thing, which is to be here. If you are not in your body, you miss the source of all significance, meaning, and satisfaction. How can you feel the satisfaction, if you aren't here? We miss who we are, which is fundamentally beingness, existence. If we are not here, we exist only on the fringes of reality. We don't sufficiently value simply being. Instead, we value what we want to accomplish, or what we want to possess. It is our biggest mistake. It is called the "great betrayal."

We are always looking for pleasure, frantically seeking happiness in many ways, and totally missing the simplest, most fundamental pleasure, which actually is also the greatest pleasure: just being here. When we are really present, the presence itself is made out of fullness, contentment, and blissful pleasure.

Our habits and conditioning lead us to forget the greatest treasure we have, our birthright—the pleasure and lightness of existence. We think that we will have pleasure or delight if we fulfill a certain plan, if a certain dream comes true, if someone we care for likes us, if we take a wonderful trip. This attitude is an insult to who we are. We *are* the pleasure, we are the joy, we are the most profound significance and the highest value. When we understand this, we see that it's ridiculous to think that we will get pleasure and joy through these external things—by doing this or that, or receiving approval or love from this or that person. We see then that we have been misinformed; we have been barking up the wrong tree.

Happiness, value, and pleasure are not the result of anything. These qualities are part of our fundamental nature. If we simply allow ourselves to be, this is our natural experience. You are the most precious thing in the universe, but you behave as if you are the poorest, most trivial thing there is. It doesn't really take much to see this. Just stop the whirlwind that goes on. Let yourself relax and be there. You can allow yourself to do it wherever you are. You don't have to be in the Canary Islands to be happy. You don't have to be with someone you are in love with, and who loves you, to be happy. Putting these conditions on your happiness is a degrading way of looking at yourself. Sure, you can be happy in the Canaries or with someone you love, but how about the rest of the time?

You abandon yourself, then start looking for satisfaction. You feel that something's missing, so you are always searching, becoming more and more frantic as all the things you acquire or accomplish don't fill you. This whole pattern occurs because you have stopped being. If you just let yourself be there, there is nowhere to go, nothing to look for, because it's all there. It is not that some people are satisfied by being and others not; no, we all feel satisfied when we are ourselves. It is a quality of our human nature. It is our natural endowment. It is the meaning of being a human being. The only thing we need do is to let ourselves be.

If you simply feel yourself at this moment, even if you don't feel your being in a full, satisfying way, you will naturally become aware of what is blocking your being. What is stopping me from being at this moment? Why do I want to go somewhere else? Why am I always thinking about what's going to make me happy? We can become naturally curious, and begin to unravel the beliefs, hopes and fears that create the blocks to being aware of our being.

When we stop to consider, we recognize that happiness is not something we're going to get somewhere, nor is it the result of some action we take. The very fabric of our beingness is itself what we are always actually looking for. We seek pleasure, joy, happiness, peace, strength, power. But these are simply aspects of our existence. Our nature, our origin is the most precious thing there is. The existence itself is a delight. This existence, this delight, is the very center of reality, all the time.

Because we forget our origin and our true nature, we tend to stay on the fringes of existence and never let ourselves live in and from the center of ourselves. It's quite a tragic story. When teachers tell you that you are asleep, or have gone astray, they mean that you have gone astray from your existence. You are asleep to your beingness. But it's not exactly that you have gone astray in the sense that you were somewhere else, lost, and now you're here. Actually, you were here all the time. You have actually always been here, but you kept looking elsewhere. Your beingness is what senses, what looks, what feels.

We are a beingness, not a thought following another thought. We are something much more fundamental, more substantial than that. We are a beingness, an existence, a presence that impregnates the present and fills our body. We go so far away from ourselves, but what we are looking for is so near. We constantly put our attention on whether the situation is what we want or don't want. Is it good or bad? But the significance of any experience is our mere presence, nothing else. The content of any experience is simply an external manifestation of that central presence.

So what is the point of waiting? What exactly are you waiting for? Is somebody going to give you what you always wanted? Will a train come from Heaven bringing you goodies? But nothing that could ever happen could be as good, as precious, as who you are.

What stops you from being, from being present, is nothing but your hope for the future. Hoping for something to be different keeps you looking for some future fantasy. But it is a mirage; you'll never get there. The mirage stops you from seeing the obvious, the preciousness of Being. It is a great distortion, a great misunderstanding of what will fulfill you. When you follow the mirage you are rejecting yourself.

Of course, when you let yourself be, as you let yourself sink into reality, you might experience unpleasant things; but these are simply the barriers that stop you from being. In time, with presence, they will dissolve. You might experience discomfort, fear, hurt, various negative feelings. These are the things that you're trying to avoid by not being here. But they are just accumulations of what has been swept under the rug of unconsciousness; they are not you. They are what you confront on the way to beingness. When we acknowledge and understand these feelings while being present, they dissolve, because the idea of ourselves that they are based on is not real.

When the illusions dissolve, what is real, your nature, will surface and remain. You go through a process of purification, not because Being itself is sullied, but because you have so many accumulated assumptions and beliefs about reality. If you continue to hope, and tell yourself stories, you will remain asleep, because reality is still the way it is whether you like it or not. The mirage hasn't worked for you yet and it will not work with more persistence. Would you want it any other way? Would you want your happiness to depend on something other than your nature?

Our work here is not to get somewhere or to accomplish something, but to allow our being to emerge. Just inhabit your body. We're not talking about something you do once in a while, when you meditate, and the rest of the time you do the important things in your life. That's how we think: "I'll meditate now, and then get on with my day, get on with my important agenda." What's important? You're important. You don't need to do anything important to be important. You don't have to achieve enlightenment or accomplish any noble action to give importance to your life. You are. That is the most important thing there is. You're very special, always. You are not important because someone thinks you're special, nor because of any unusual capacities or accomplishments. You are important because of your nature; you cannot help being important and precious. Nothing can prove it or disprove it.

You are important because without your actual presence, there is no significance in life, no value in life. When you are conscious of your existence the experience is unmitigated pleasure. This pleasure is there regardless of what you're doing—scrubbing floors, going to the bathroom, creating something wonderful. Every moment is precious, and lived to the fullest. You are not the feelings or the thoughts or the content of your awareness. None of these are who you are. You are the fullness of your Being, the substance of your presence.

THREE

Who am I?

Some time ago I asked the question, "Why are you here?" On another occasion I asked, "Are you here?" I don't know whether you've stayed with those questions and investigated them for yourself. Today I'm going to ask a third question which is a natural progression from those: "Who are you?"

The answer to this question is not a statement, so if one is conjured up in your mind, disregard it. We are going to explore whether it is possible to answer the question, "Who am I?" I'm not going to give you answers, but I will help guide the exploration by asking you questions, and you can investigate while we are talking.

You always say "I am …" and "I want. …" so we want to see what "I" is. We are not implying from the outset that there is such a thing as an "I." We don't want to begin with assumptions. So we are not assuming that there is an answer, or that there is one answer, or that there is no answer. We are not assuming that if there is an answer, it can be said in words. We want to be open to all the possibilities. We want to ask the question in complete openness, in a complete absence of assumptions. This investigation will be based purely on our curiosity and on our interest in finding the truth. What is the truth that is here for you?

You may find that when you ask, "Who am I?" something comes to your mind like, "I am the the one who has done this," or "I'm 5'4" and weigh 130 lbs." Statements, images, and sensations may pop into your mind. We are not saying that these are not you; we want to investigate whether they are or not.

We are not assuming that a self can be found, or that if it can be found, that it can be described. We want to investigate who you are—if there really is such a thing; and if there is, what it is, and if it can be known. You probably think "Of course, I have a self, and I know what it is, or if I don't, I will sometime." So I'm telling you, don't assume that. You say, "Wait a minute, what's left?" Nothing's left—that's the point.

You notice we use the words "I" and "self" and we think, feel, and behave as if there is something here that is our "self." We already have a feeling or a sense that there is a selfhood, that there is a me-ness. Now we want to investigate what that sense of self is about. What is that sense of being a person, a self, an identity? What are you referring to when you say "I am," "I want," "I like," "I do," or "I don't"?

You may have had an experience in the past and felt, "That's me." Maybe you were right, maybe not. Even if it's true that you recognized yourself then, perhaps now you have a different self. We want to know what you experience now. We want to be right here, right at this moment. Let's investigate our beliefs, rather than taking them for granted. When you have experienced what you perceive as your true self, it's not unusual to think, "I've experienced myself and that's it, now I'll be happy forever after." Well, maybe, but we want to know right now. Can you answer the question definitely, you yourself at this very moment, when you say, "Who am I?"

One thing that can help our investigation is to connect the feeling of "I," the feeling of self, to what is called "identity" or "identification." Finding out who you are is essentially finding your identity. You can see the connection between identity and identification, if you look at your experience of any moment, and see that at that very moment you are identifying with something, you're taking yourself to be something in particular. You might not be consciously aware of what you are taking yourself to be, but at any moment you are taking yourself to be something, or someone.

So we want to investigate what or who you are taking yourself to be at each moment and question it. Is that really who you are? At each moment there is an identification, there is, in a sense, a feeling of self: "I am watching," or "I am sitting." When you say "I," that "I" is attached to something. Is what you're attaching the "I" to really you?

When you are meditating, for instance, who is meditating? Who is sitting at this moment? Be aware of your experience. See whether you can answer that question. What is it you attach the "I" to? Who am I that is sitting? Most likely you'll see that you attach the "I" to your body. It's the body that is sitting, so when you say "I am sitting," aren't you saying "I am the body"? You're not taking yourself to be a feeling or a perception, because feelings don't sit, the mind doesn't walk. The only part that sits, walks, and moves is the body.

We find that the identification with the body is powerful and consistent. It is much subtler and deeper than we usually imagine it to be. Of course, some people can't imagine anything else—"What else could I be?" It's not easy to disidentify from the body because all our lives we've been taking ourselves to be the body. I'm not saying that you need to do anything to change this; you just need to be aware that this is the case. Are you really aware that you're taking yourself to be the body?

When we say "my body," what does the body belong to? Saying "myself" is more accurate, but what exactly does that mean? Who is it who has a body and has a self? Who are you referring to when you say "I have a body"? What is the "I"? It doesn't make sense to say "I have an I" or "self has a self." Is there a big self who has a small self?

Are you getting confused? That's good. You are confused, and all this time you thought you knew. One reason for this investigation is to show you that you really don't know.

See yourself now, sitting and looking. Who is looking? Just observe yourself now, you sitting and looking. What is looking? What do you experience? You say, "Well, I'm looking through my eyes and thinking in my head." What is looking through your eyes? What is thinking in your head? What are you taking yourself to be?

You are a presence sitting there. What is the presence you are experiencing? Does it have a shape? Most likely you'll see right away that the shape of your presence seems to be the shape of your body; even if you don't take your body to be you, at least the shape of your body is defining who you are. We're not implying that this identification is bad or wrong. We don't know. We just want to investigate—is it true?

You can pursue this by looking at your present experience. What is "you"? Experientially, at this very moment, what is it you take yourself to be? If you become aware that you're taking yourself to be the body, the awareness of the identification usually leads to disidentification. You begin to see that maybe you are not the body. What are you then?

If you're not taking yourself to be the body at this moment, what are you taking yourself to be? You might feel a sense of identity, or a sense of entity. What is this sense? You might associate it with your mind. "There seems to be a feeling of self, and it seems to be inside my body, but it is not my body itself." What is the you that has a self? Is it a feeling? Is it a sensation? Is it a thought or a stream of thoughts you are calling "self"? Is it an emotional or mental reaction that you call "I"? Or is it something connected to the past? Are you taking yourself to be all that happened to you in the past?

Memories are the normal way of defining yourself: "I was born on such and such a date, to these parents, under this sign, etc. My mother abandoned me; my mother loved me. I went to school, didn't like it, and got A's anyway. I didn't have sex until I was 21, so I was frustrated. I got pregnant and had an abortion. I was married but it didn't last, and so on." Right? You define yourself that way. Can you imagine yourself, describe yourself, without using those memories?

All these things that have happened, the whole collection of them, are not separate from what you take yourself to be. The mental sense of identity and the emotional sense of self are indistinguishable from everything that has happened to you. It is as if all that has happened in your life—all the events, feelings, emotions, reactions, good and bad experiences, your whole history—are inseparable from what you take yourself to be now. In fact, that is how you usually know yourself.

But what does who you are have to do with your history? The personal history happened to your body. When you say, "I was hit by a car," what was hit by a car? When you say, "I was abandoned," what do you take to be abandoned by your mother? "I was born," what was born? You relate all these events, all these memories to your body. This body is moving through time and space, and all these things are happening to it. So either you take the body itself as you, or you take what has happened to it and form an amorphous construct, a kind of psychological identity, that determines your present sense of identity. And somehow you feel it will determine your future.

So now you may be aware of identifying with that personal history and its collective sense of selfhood. All this has a tag that you call "me." What is this tag? When you take the personal history to define you, all of your experiences are included, even experiences of self-realization, enlightenment, and Essence. You also use these memories to define you. For instance, you might remember an experience that you had about two months ago in which you experienced your true self, and now you think that must be you. It became food for your personal history. You're trying to generate an identity now by remembering it. Who says that is who you are now? Are you always the same? When you take a memory to define you, it doesn't matter what you remember—good, bad, fundamental, superficial, true or false; it all accumulates in your personal history. Even an experience of your true self can be remembered and added to the collection. But your true self is not an accumulation or a collection.

Mysterious, isn't it? Now you might say, "Wait a minute. If I am not the body, and I'm not my sense of personal history, who am I then? I'm on the verge of something." When you say, "I'm on the verge of something," you wonder: "Is it to be scared of or longed for? Should I hope for it; should I fear it? Should I go toward it, or resist it?" Well, who are you at this moment? Aren't you identifying with your personal history? And doesn't that personal history want to have one more experience to know for sure who it is?

Suppose I could tell you who you really are. What difference would it make? What if I say, "Yes, you have a self, and it feels like such and such, and it does such and such." So what? It is simply one more piece of information to put in your mind and add to your personal history. It's not even an experience—it's a memory that's not even yours.

Is it possible to look not only at your body and see your identification with it, but also to look objectively at your personal history without having to identify with it? Is it possible to look at the totality of your personality at once? Most of the time you identify with that totality; you are in the middle of it, as if in a medium like a cloud, and you let the atmosphere of that cloud define you. Is it possible to become aware that you are doing that? Can you look at your experience right now and see how you are identifying with your personal history? Are you aware of how hard it is to disengage from those thoughts and memories and ideas about yourself?

Don't try to disengage. Just be aware of how you are not disengaging. We are not trying to do anything, we're just trying to see. We just want to see what is really there. And all I'm doing is guiding you to look here and here and here. That's all. As I said, we are exploring. We don't necessarily assume that there is a definite answer or that the answer can even be found. We're just exploring, and so far I haven't told you anything.

When you look at the totality that way, you will see that there are patterns that seem to be unchanging. You've always thought of yourself as the same person. You may have changed a little—maybe you like different things, maybe you're happier; but you're generally the same. You still think the same way. You still feel similar feelings, or you react to things the same way that you've reacted to them before. Personal history has a vague sort of consistency and continuity that gives us a sense of identity. The sense of identity is nothing but a tag, a feeling that comes from a collection of memories.

It is a little like a movie. If you look at a movie, it seems continuous, but when you stop it, you see that there is one picture here, one picture here, and so on. Your memories are a series of pictures, just like the movies. They are pictures put together and moving so you have a sense of continuity, which you use for self-definition. Your personal history defines who you are, what you're about; in fact, it defines what you feel like now, and what you will do when you stop this investigation.

Do you see how hard it is to disengage from this? You can't allow yourself to say, "Well, maybe I don't have to be defined by that. Maybe I don't have to know where I'm going when I leave this room," because then you think, "Wait a minute. I'll be lost. I'll lose my memory and they'll have to take me to the hospital and give me drugs to remind me who I am. So I'd better hold on to my memories, my identity. Now I'm oriented; I know who I am and so I'm safe." But how can anything new happen? Whatever is going to happen is already determined by these things.

Perhaps you are smart and say, "I know I do that, but I know better. I know I'm not really my personal history. I'm experiencing an essential state now; it feels wonderful, like a kind of love. That must be me, right?" If you are taking these states to be you, just pay attention. Be aware of what you are taking yourself to be. Is this essential state what you were feeling an hour ago? If it wasn't there, who were you then? Essence manifests in different ways. Maybe an hour ago you were another aspect. The only thing you really know is that you are remembering one experience, and now there is a different experience. What makes you think that is who you are? A few moments from now you will experience something else.

For instance, you may say, "I'm really unhappy these days, or I'm feeling angry." What do you mean? Are these statements accurate? Is there an "I" that is feeling these things? Yes, your body has feelings and sensations of unhappiness, and your mind has ideas and associations of unhappiness, but why do you assume that you are unhappy? Maybe you think that you are your feelings. Are you really angry, or simply aware of anger in the body and mind? Don't speculate, simply look at what is there.

So we see that at different times you take your body to be you, or a feeling to be you, or an essential aspect to be you. Your sense of identity keeps changing its tag. Who you are taking yourself to be shifts all the time. The content is changing, but you're always saying "I" as if the "I" were one thing.

Is it possible to be aware of the whole process? Is it possible to be aware that now I am identified with my body, now with a thought, now with a memory, now with my feeling—to be aware of the process of shifting the attachment of identity to all these things? If that is what we are doing, why not investigate it?

Does that mean that there is no "I," there is no real self? Is it just a matter of identification, just attachment to one thing after another with no continuity? If that is the case, then there is no self, no you, and no "I," only strings of events, attachments, and identifications. That could be the answer. But let's see whether there are other possibilities. We are seeing that it is possible for our awareness, our consciousness, to expand to include more and more.

When you attach your sense of identity to something in particular, how are you doing it? What is really happening? When you feel that you are the body, penetrate the feeling. What are you doing that causes you to take the body to be you? Why not simply feel that there is a body? Why say "I am my body"? What is happening when you say, "I am sitting and talking," instead of "I am aware of a body sitting and talking." What is happening there? And you do the same thing with your personal history, with your psychological sense of identity. Why not say, "Yes, there is a perception or there is a memory," instead of saying, "That's me"?

How is the identification happening? We need to observe the process of attachment; we need to observe the process of labeling. When we explore these questions, we find a process of thought that involves concepts. There is a concept of self, of identity, that we feel we need. There are also tensions in the body that accompany that thinking process. And the tensions in the body, the thinking process, and the sense of attachment to our identity go together; they are inseparable.

Now, it is possible to be aware of that process of thinking and the process of holding on, and thus the pattern of tensions in the body without having to change any of it. Instead of defining ourselves with these thoughts, tensions, and sensations, why not look at them as a totality, as an awareness, rather than as a limitation or self-definition? So that there is an awareness watching the thought processes and associations, physical and emotional, but not necessarily involved with them. What can look at the totality of our thinking processes, the tensions in the body, the emotions, the body itself, the body image, the self-image, the personal history, everything? What is it that can look? What can hold all of that?

It's not a matter of thinking about it. If you're thinking about it, just be aware that you are thinking about it. It's not a matter of visualizing it. If you begin to visualize, just be aware of the attempt to visualize. And so you will see by following your awareness that if it is not possible for you to be aware of the totality, it is because there are thoughts that you are involved in. You're stuck in certain thoughts, stuck in certain tensions that hold you in the middle of the whole thing. I'm not asking you to look at what is looking, but simply to be aware of everything at once—the totality. Even the part that wants to look—is it a thought, a tension in the body, a memory?

Is it possible to look, not only at yourself at the present time, but to look at the whole span of time, your whole life? Is it possible to have a general sense that there is a whole life which, from the beginning until now, has continuity? What is it that holds all of that?

Can you disengage from that history, from whatever identification you have right now, by being aware of the identification? Are you at this moment identifying yourself with the part of you that wants to know what I am saying? When you are aware of this, is your awareness of the whole situation coming from within your body? Is there something inside your body that's looking out? If your attention is looking from within the body, is it possible to disengage from that, to be aware that you are attaching yourself to being inside your body?

If we continue this investigation, we see that some of our identifications are limited by our ideas of time, and some of them are limited by our ideas of space. We use time and space to define ourselves. Is that needed? What will happen if you don't use time and space to define yourself? If you don't use your personal history? If you don't use your ideas about inside, outside, big, small, and so on? What if you just become aware of the movement of restricting yourself within the body, aware of making yourself big or small, inside or outside the body?

Your thoughts may be going very fast right now. Be aware of the thought process. This is not a matter of thinking. The thought process is determined by your personal history. But it is possible to be aware of what we are talking about. So if you don't try to make up an identity by using your body, by using your feelings, thoughts, memories, or the idea of space and time, what happens?

This is not a matter of knowing something by being able to name it; it's a matter of simply being aware of what we're talking about. You don't need to make any decisions; you don't need to remember anything. You don't need any work you've done in the past. You don't need anything. We are just looking at the situation in this moment. It's not a matter of freeing yourself from anything; it's not a matter of doing anything. It's not a matter of having any particular experience. We're exploring what you mean when you say "I."

Now, when we see all these things, is there still a sense of "I" left? What are you attaching the "I" to at this moment? And if you are not attaching the "I" to anything, can you see the totality of your universe—anything you've ever thought, felt, experienced, conceived of—all of it together? Can you see the whole universe that you take to be you?

You put yourself in a form, in a package, and that limits you. If you can see the package from all sides, obviously you are not what's inside the package. If you can allow this perception to happen, then it is possible that you may see that you are beyond all that. You may see that your universe does not define you and must not define you. At the moment that you are defined by that universe, or any content in it, you're trapped. You are in the middle; you are in it. You are at the mercy of all the forces within that personal universe. If you allow yourself to see the whole, then it is possible to see that you are really none of it. There is no need to attach yourself to that universe or any part of it, nor to define yourself by it or any part of it. And it is possible for that universe to continue in whatever way it continues without your having to take it to be you.

Just the mere fact that there is the possibility of a complete awareness of the totality indicates that it doesn't have to define you. Just the mere fact that you can contain the whole thing, and still your capacity is not exhausted, indicates that you are bigger than all that. The moment you become aware of something is the moment of going beyond it. The moment you say, "I am that," you are beyond it.

When we believe our labels, when our identity is any content, we are defining ourselves and not allowing expansion beyond that idea of ourselves. The moment I say, "I was born at such and such a time," I define myself with the body. But if I realize that I am using my birth to indicate the beginning of my life, I can see that the "I" wasn't born at all. How can something that can be aware of this whole totality be born? How can it die? What does it have to do with time?

So are we finding an answer? Are we finding out the answer to "Who am I?" Or are we finding that every time we say, "That is me," we are not that, because our awareness can include it. What we're finding is a paradoxical, contradictory kind of answer. It is neither finding, nor not finding an answer.

We're only exposing things that you think you know. If you're getting confused, that's good, because the confusion is there anyway. You have been covering it up by believing that you know. At this moment, you probably don't know who you are.

For a long time you have said out of habit, "I'm sitting or getting up, talking, feeling sad." But are these statements accurate? If you question these assumptions, you may wonder why you keep saying these things. Why do I keep saying that? Who is saying that? What is this "I"? You see it must be inaccurate. When you look at things this way, you'll see that you've been confused all these years.

You may ask, "So what have I been doing all this time?" You may feel you have been wasting your time, but what are you taking yourself to be that's been wasting your time? The moment you say that "I" have been doing anything, you are making assumptions about an "I." There's no need to think about what you've done and haven't done, since what you think "you" have done depends on what you thought you were. The past is completely irrelevant. Completely.

Knowing the answer to "Who am I?" happens only in the moment. The answer has nothing to do with the past. If the past determines the answer now, then it is obviously not a correct answer, since the past no longer exists. To really answer the question requires that we see that we don't know, and also that we don't know how to find out. Is it possible to let yourself see that you don't know the answer and don't know how to find it, and still let the question burn in you? "Who am I?"

"Who am I?"

Can we allow ourselves to see that we don't know? If we assume we know, then we stop the inquiry. If we assume we know how to go about it, we assume we know what the answer is, that we know what we are looking for. Perhaps not knowing is the real knowing. If you allow yourself to see that you don't really know and you don't know how to know, something can happen. Maybe this is your first chance of really knowing something. Assuming that you know and assuming that you know what to do are barriers to true knowing. When you finally know that you don't know, you finally have absolute knowledge. Complete ignorance is what will bring true knowledge.

You see, the mind can't function here. This has nothing to do with your mind. Your mind can only answer the question and say that some of the answers are not the answers. The only thing we can do is to eliminate what we believe we know and see that we really don't know. That's all we can do. We cannot do anything positive to begin finding out because the moment we do that we're assuming that we know where we're going. How do you know what should happen? That knowledge is inferred from memory, from past experience.

When you see that you don't know and don't know how to know, you may stop all the activities that you do to try to know, and then maybe something will happen. Maybe there is a possibility of a different kind of knowing, a knowing that is completely fresh. It's also possible that the knowing will just be that you don't know. Maybe you'll just know that you are not defined by anything that you usually define yourself with, and that there's no way to define yourself. You may only know that you're undefinable, and that knowing you are undefinable is freedom. So maybe that is the final definition of you. But this is an experience, a realization, and not merely a logical conclusion.

This is a very personal sort of question. It's intimately your question. It's not theoretical, nor is it something you can answer just by thinking. It's not something that someone else can answer for you. It must become your own personal concern. And whatever happens as you are investigating the question, you need only to be aware of it. You don't need to come to conclusions. It's an open-ended investigation. And whatever you find, you needn't formulate in words.

Any questions?

Student: It sounds like you're saying that you feel that freedom is inversely proportional to one's definition of oneself.

A.H. Almaas: Yes; when you define yourself, you restrict yourself. The fact of defining indicates that there is something bigger than the definition.

S: I find that every couple of years I want to go to a foreign country with only a small pack. It's like I'm taking a break from myself, and it feels very free.

AH: That's an attempt to get some distance from your personal history. Many people feel that they want to take a break from themselves. That's why many people take vacations. But you see, although changing physical space can help a little, the important thing is to get out of the personal history, and you take that with you in your mind.

Many people feel that need, and try to get distance from their personal lives in many ways. One of the ways is going to the movies or being immersed in a novel. Why do people go to the movies? To escape, take a mini-vacation from themselves. You go to some dramatic movie, get completely involved and forget all about your life. You're completely someone else. That's the vacation; then when the movie's over, you come right back.

What we're talking about here is much more radical. To really answer this question is to be completely outside and uninfluenced by your personal history. This can only happen by a radical transformation inside—by actually seeing directly that you are not it, not just by trying to get out of it.

S: I guess my little matrix of problems is another definition of myself, and so I go to a foreign country to take a break from them and get a whole new set of problems to deal with instead.

AH: Right. You're defining yourself as a person who has problems, who needs to take a vacation from problems. So you change one personal history for another. That doesn't resolve it, but gives a little relief for a moment.

All these attempts, including the Work, are simply a rearrangement of personal history, so that we can see it as a totality. Most of the time our personal history is arranged so that we are totally enmeshed in it. By doing the Work, we rearrange the pieces so that we can look at it. When you look at it, it is possible to see beyond it.

The Work helps you to see the pieces, and the more you do it, the bigger the pieces you see, and the bigger the picture you see, until you can see the whole thing. When that happens, it's possible to see that there is something beyond all of this.

S: I think I came into the Work to escape my claustrophobia and stuckness.

AH: You want to be unstuck, right? But when you want to be unstuck, you're defining yourself as a person who is stuck. Maybe when you look at yourself as somebody who is stuck, that makes you stuck. It's part of the personal history—to be somebody who is stuck. I'm not saying that you don't feel that way; I'm saying look at it a different way.

S: Are you saying that each time you see a totality, it becomes another piece, and each time you see that piece, it expands again?

AH: No, not necessarily. I'm saying that every time you define a totality, you go beyond it. If you define the beyond, you may go beyond it, but beyond means not defined.

S: I can't picture "going beyond" unless I die. To me, everything you're talking about is what happens to people when they die and leave their body.

AH: That means you're identifying with your body, right? Because you say, "... unless I die," but what is it that dies? You see? So just see that you identify with your body, and that's why you feel that you can't get beyond it. I'm saying that it is possible to disidentify without dying.

Language is tricky. You have to be aware of your language, because it can trap you. If you believe what you are saying, you are trapped. The moment you say, "... unless I die," and believe it, you are trapped. You are thinking about the body. Of course, you need to use your name, birth date, and so on, for practical things, but that's the only reason you need an identity. It's not needed psychologically. And it's not needed for your existence.

S: What good does it do to find out who I am? Why even try to do it?

AH: It doesn't do the real self any good. It doesn't change the real self. But for your mind, it makes all the difference because your mind can't rest until it finds out. For me, knowing myself doesn't make a difference because the real self is always there. But for my body and my mind, there is more rest, there is more peace, there is more pleasure, and there is more relaxation, when there is a knowingness that I am beyond all of that.

Whether it does any good is completely irrelevant. The question is there by the mere fact that you don't know. That question is a statement, and the statement is that you don't know who you are. You can't not know who you are and not have the question. It's impossible. You can pretend to know in order to silence the question for a while, but as long as you don't know, the question is always there. We often try to numb ourselves to the discontent that goes along with the question. You can do this only at great expense—a lessening of life.

People want so much to stop the question, to silence it. There are two motivations behind that desire: not wanting to suffer, and the deeper motivation that the question has to be answered. The question is there because you don't know the answer. And it's going to stay there; it will stay with you until it's answered. It has a force of its own. That's a fact. It's one of the natural laws. The questioning is always there, until there is finally no question.

FOUR

The Chasm

Each of us has a central need: to find meaning in our lives. This drive may not be apparent; it might not even be conscious. But if you examine the situation, you will see the influence of this drive in most of the activities and concerns in your life. Philosophy, especially twentieth century philosophy in the form of existentialism and phenomenology, is largely concerned with the question of emptiness and meaninglessness in life. I think that this concern in philosophy, as well as in literature and the arts, reflects increasing general awareness of the issue of meaning.

Sometimes an individual directly questions the meaning of life. But most of the time people are preoccupied with activities and endeavors that they assume will give meaning and significance to their lives. Rarely do we come to the

35

point of questioning, because we are usually trying to pretend that we know the answer already. People create all kinds of goals which they hope will give meaning to their lives. These goals generally involve future plans for accomplishments such as being creative, successful, rich, able to travel, to win, etc.

Remember the song, "What's it all about, Alfie? Is it just for the moment we live?" Maybe so. Perhaps it is just for the moment we live. Philosophy is an attempt to answer this question. Ultimately philosophy can be seen as the science of meaning; yet the question of the meaning of life is not merely an intellectual exercise. When a person is really questioning his life, it doesn't feel intellectual. It feels as if life has no value, no worth, no point. Even if we are not aware of this issue, we are engaged with it all the time, even in the course of our daily activities. Although we have other concerns, this one is central and often underlies our apparent concerns.

Another way to look at the question, "What is the point of life?" might be, "What is the significance of life? Why do I do what I do every day? What is the point of waking up in the morning, going to the bathroom, brushing my teeth, washing myself, having breakfast, going to work, talking to people, coming home, eating dinner, having a good time, going to sleep? Every day I do these things. Why? One day is enough if I want to experience these things: I only need to eat once to know what it's like to eat. So why do I continue? What's in it for me?"

I am asking a fundamental question for you to ponder, so that when this issue arises in you, you might stay with the question without dismissing it with a superficial answer. For a person to arrive at this issue of meaning, he must already be disappointed in his life, either by having reached his goals or by having been disappointed in his dreams. "My mother wanted me to marry a doctor, and my father wanted me to be successful, and I did it. I have two kids and everything

I thought I wanted. But nothing is resolved; I still feel the same way. I'm still waiting, looking for something. I've done the things I set out to do and I'm not satisfied."

This is often the time when a person begins to question, when the dreams have been played out but there is no contentment. Or perhaps you thought about these questions in college, when your teachers or parents were living it out and becoming disillusioned. So your teacher brings up this question, and you get interested intellectually; it sounds interesting. You're young, you want to know about everything, or maybe you just want to get an "A" in the meaning of life.

So you finish school, and go about getting your family together, your work, your successes, your ideals, whatever they are. Some people never fulfill their ideals or actualize their plans, so they're still hoping the big triumph will happen. Perhaps they are even postponing success so that they won't have to face the awareness that it does not fulfill them. If they never complete their goals, they won't have to question the meaning of their lives. A few lucky people do accomplish their dreams, and this question naturally arises for them. If they are sensitive, they are then not easily distracted from this question.

It is difficult to convince someone who still has dreams, plans, and ideals that have not been accomplished, that the issue of meaning is important and that it has nothing to do with these things, accomplished or not. This is the reason that in the old times in Work schools people were accepted only in the mature phases of life. Younger people were not believed capable of giving up on the hope that achieving their dreams would satisfy them, unless perhaps they were disappointed very early.

As you have probably observed, most of us are still like that, still hoping this or that plan will give it to us. There is nothing wrong with having kids, family, a job, certain ideals to live up to. But, these things don't answer the question of meaning. They have different purposes: they are entertaining, fill your stomach, warm your bed, give you company and intimacy, provide something to be occupied with. But they don't provide you the meaning of life.

Many things determine whether you confront this essential question. It depends on how intelligent you are, how much experience you have had in your life, your early upbringing, many things. And people use many ploys and distractions to avoid confronting this question.

Sometimes a person will dedicate twenty to forty years of effort, with all his heart and energy, to accomplishing a goal. He is driven to fulfill his ideals. He doesn't need to achieve this goal in order to survive or to satisfy his actual needs. So what does his success give him? Maybe a little more money than he had before. But is that what drives him? Is that what success is for? "Well, it will make me feel better about myself, make me feel good, make me feel worthy." So, it gives a kind of significance, importance and meaning to his life, and that is the driving force. We idealize certain things, and then believe these ideals will give meaning and significance to our activities. In order to feel that what we are doing is significant, we cling to an ideal, project perfection on the future, and work toward it.

So the quest for significance, for the feeling that the life we are living is worthwhile, is the real basis of all our dreams. When you join a Work group, your ideal might become self-realization. This is still something you are working toward to give you meaning. A career might serve this function for a person, or it can be a relationship, or a lover. It can be a creative or artistic activity or project. Exercising any of one's capacities—thinking capacities, physical capacities, creative capacities—can serve our quest for meaning.

What I'm talking about is not unusual or hidden. If you ask someone, "What does your career give you?" he is likely to say, "Oh, it gives me excitement, a sense of purpose in my life." This is what people believe; it is what is accepted in our society.

Of course, there are other ways of avoiding the sense of lack of meaning. Many people depend on some kind of stimulation, or stimulating activities to seek out intense sensations. Examples of this are getting involved in dangerous activities such as sports, crime, or drugs. So there is a sense of intense sensation, strong stimulations, that can give one a sense that, "Yes, I exist, there is something there, my life is happening; it's not just empty and meaningless." Others tend not to go toward the intense sensations but try to avoid the whole issue by numbing themselves, becoming dull and asleep. People spend years, even whole lives, living on the surface of themselves.

Those who deal with the drive for meaning by pursuing various goals and activities are actually also numbing the drive, by believing that they are fulfilling it or engaged in fulfilling it.

The activities through which we seek meaning are usually very hard to let go of, because our deep need to have something to think about, something to do, becomes as intense as the drive itself. Some people worry all the time, because they can't stand the feeling that they wouldn't know what to do if the activity stopped. As long as we have a goal, even something like wanting to heal an ache in the body, there is meaning in our lives. The meaning of my life might consist of trying to fix my hurt knee. Some people look for the meaning of their lives in their children. Many mothers can't find meaning in their own lives so they try to live through their children.

You see how pervasive this issue is. Even when we are engaged in activities that give us real pleasure and joy, we are always hoping that they will also give meaning and importance to our lives. You believe that if you live in a certain way, your life will not be empty. Perhaps you feel that if you really confront the meaninglessness and emptiness, it might be too much to bear. And it is true that we cannot live without meaning in our lives, without a sense of significance, of worth, value, and importance. So we try to find substitutes for it. The activities are not wrong or bad; it is just that they are weighed down by unrealistic expectations. A child is burdened with its mother's need to live through it. A creative endeavor is not the same when it is used to fill the need for significance. It becomes burdened by distraction, avoidance, and suppression.

Ultimately, the desire for meaning and significance is a search for identity. Our activities are meant to give us a sense of who we are. "What gives me significance?" When we explore this we find that it has something to do with a sense of self. "Who am I? I'm the minister of the church (or a doctor, or the wife of such and such a person, etc.)" Although we may dismiss these roles as just social convention and not ultimately important, these identities do have importance in our minds. We cling to these things to give us a sense of identity and security. Even our relationships with people give us a sense of who we are, as if they were mirrors. Or perhaps my success seems to reflect my worth to me. I believe that if I achieve my goal, then I have become something. We all try to become somebody, to live up to a certain image. For some it's the image of helping others as a doctor, a teacher, a lawyer, a leader, a therapist, a perfect mother or father, etc. For others it is the image of a big, strong, successful business person, or the image of a sophisticate, or of a brilliant intellect. Some even take pride in their self-image as a humble saintly person, or as a seeker.

So we see that our needs for meaning and significance pervade nearly all our endeavors. You feel that you can't live your life if it's not meaningful. How can I live my life, if I don't have meaning in my life, something to give me a good sense of self and identity?

That's why some people who are very successful, famous, or rich kill themselves when it slips away, as if the money, or beauty, or fame had been the life. It's gone, so what's the point in living? Some people kill themselves or die soon after a spouse dies, as if the other had been invested with all the meaning of living. When the central thing that gives one the impetus to live goes, whether it's a relationship, a skill, or an ideal, there is a big emptiness left. Many people are surprised by how much they were invested, and beforehand would have denied that the person or accomplishment was what gave their lives meaning. But at the moment of loss, it becomes obvious. Even when people retire from a job they would have said had no meaning except for the paycheck, they often feel devastated at the loss of the activity or the role. What is actually lost is the sense of identity. The filler is taken away, so they are faced with the need to escape a sense of meaningless emptiness.

The emptiness was there all the time, but there was a cork in it. That cork was the career or relationship or ideal or philosophy or sex, whatever stimulating or distracting agent the person was using. Our whole society not only condones this substitution of external factors for intrinsic meaning, but actually idealizes it. With few exceptions, society as a whole tries to deal with the search for meaning in these ways. Even our love, our intelligence, and our body give us a sense of identity.

When we confront these perceptions we may well wonder, "If I don't do any of that, if I don't want my value to rest on anything else, what will be left?" When I get a sense of meaning from the intense sensations and identities in my life, the meaning is not intrinsic; it's still cause and effect. What if we say, "Wait a minute, I don't want the importance of my life to depend on what I do, what people think of me, even what I think of me, or on a skill I have"? What else is there? Where does the significance come from then?

The self-deception that we manage even in asking this question is amazing. Even your search for the answer can be used to give you a sense of meaning. A person can be engaged in his life seeking for meaning, with his search functioning as just another identity that is no more real or intrinsic than any other role. The world is full of seekers whose identity is wrapped up in seeking wisdom, truth, or enlightenment. This is basically the same as seeking riches, beauty, fame, love, or recognition. The purpose of all of these identifications is to fill emptiness. But if you could look at the situation with complete sincerity, if you could just see what's really there without the props, you would give yourself a little chance of finding true intrinsic meaning.

It is not easy to look clearly and sincerely at ourselves. Most of us don't even know what is difficult about it. We just find our minds dodging in all directions to avoid it. I break up with my boyfriend, and suddenly I'm eating. If I'm not eating, I'm doing my paintings that I haven't touched in ten years. Or I am just divorced or retired, so I'm going to travel for a year or so to see what's there in life. Now this may be a great idea, but what is motivating you? Our minds are clever at avoiding the feeling that arises at the end of anything, because there is a terror of having no supporting mirrors to give us meaning. Just to exist as we are brings up a big fear of the emptiness. There is usually a fear that we don't really have any Essence, and that we don't have an identity. We may believe that the emptiness is all there is. This might be reinforced by early childhood experiences involving a panic about being different from others, about being different from our parents, for example, which creates a kind of self-consciousness.

Young children are completely involved when they are playing. They are not trying to be something or accomplish something. They might be happily content with the moment, or crying about something, but they are completely in the moment. Then little by little, the child begins to do things to get someone's reaction or attention, to be good, or to get approval. The child begins to become fake, and after a while the innocence is gone. This is easy to observe when you are around a child growing up. We have forgotten that we too are like that, fake, because we have learned to be subtle and hide it, even from ourselves. But in the early years when the child says something to you, it is often obvious when there is a manipulation of their real experience or desire. They are not subtle at the early stages. As they grow up, they become more subtle and more defended against their impulses and feelings in the moment. Finally, the usual identification with the personality prevails, and we believe that everything we do is real. We have come to believe our own pretensions.

At the beginning the child seems to have a significance. This is not a mental or inferred significance. The identity of the child is not dependent on something external. Children are real, true to themselves. They have a connectedness, a oneness, rather than disharmony. The child is one entity, responding and reacting and behaving as a whole, not as this part and then that part. That happens later. There isn't even a distinction between Essence and personality. The child is simply one beingness. As the child grows older, this unity of experience is lost.

What causes the transition? Something that was there has been lost, and something that is fake has taken its place. This is what we call "false personality." If you go very deep inside yourself, you'll see that what you take yourself to be is not real. One way of experiencing this is feeling that you are an empty shell, with nothing of any significance inside. The ego identity, the core of the personality with its sense of self, can be directly felt as a dry, empty shell. When you see through the personality shell and become aware of the emptiness inside, you become aware of the sense of meaninglessness, worthlessness, and the insignificance.

We usually feel this emptiness in vague ways, rather than directly. But when we confront the situation deeply, we feel like a kind of egg shell with nothing inside. When people perceive this empty shell, they often feel, "Why should I live?" There is nothing there, no significance. Everything in the world becomes meaningless. It doesn't hold any interest. Snow falls and there is no one there to appreciate it. In such a state of meaninglessness I don't even know what it's like to appreciate something. I'm not there. How can a deficient emptiness appreciate beautiful falling snow?

In contrast, when we observe a child, we see that the sense of fullness, of intrinsic aliveness, of joy in being, is not inferred, that is, it is not the result of something else. There is value in just being oneself; it is not because of something one does or doesn't do. It is there at the beginning but slowly gets lost, and the fakeness just takes over.

It is lost, but not easily. The child puts up a great fight, a tremendous struggle, but at some point he gives up. At some point we feel that the conflict between our real sense of ourselves and our environment is too much to take. The child is not seen, or he feels rejected, not valued, or not related to. It is very lonely to be real amidst all the normal falsehood of personality. Eventually, it is too much to bear. There is no support for being ourselves; the true self is not valued by our parents. They might value what we do, how cute we look, but they are not really there themselves. Perhaps they are busy with the push for success. As a young child, that's not how we feel. "Strange, I don't know how to connect with all of that—there's just me, that's it. I'm just sitting here playing with my toy, what more is there? But, look at these adults, what are they doing? I feel alone, but I can't say these things to any of the people around me. Mommy wants me to do this, and I want Mommy to hold me so I'd better do what she wants."

That's the moment of the great betrayal, when we abandon ourselves. Like the person in the story, "The King's

Son," we begin to live like the natives live. We put on the robes, and the robes are made of fakeness. That fakeness is the shell we feel. It is the fabric of the shell. What is real in us has been pushed away, and all our lives we feel the shell. If we penetrate the shell, we feel the emptiness. This predicament is very sad, but it is universal. It happens to everyone who identifies with the ego sense of self, with the usual personality. One is either oneself, as essential Being, or one is a self of ego, developed over time, which is an empty shell. When we confront this shell, we are touched in the deepest place. We are in deep anguish, because what would make life meaningful is not there. One may feel then, "I want to be totally here, nothing else will do it. Nothing has significance, even pleasure and essential experience, if I am not here." But we do not want to confront this, because we don't want to feel now the abandonment and alienation we felt as children.

Your parents' failure to see your real nature does not mean that they do not love you. Even if they love you, are nice to you, provide for you, and even think you are wonderful, it is not the same as actually seeing who you are. Even people who have good parents will still develop this fake shell. The most original you, your center, your spark was not seen; it was not recognized, not responded to, and often it was disapproved of and rejected. If your parents don't have their own center, their own deep sense of self, they can't see you. They can see in you only what they see in themselves, regardless of how much they want the best for you and love you. Even if they were to glimpse the real center of you, they would have to defend against this perception, because it would make them feel their own lack. So we could call this phenomenon of identifying with the shell a social disease that has been transmitted through the ages.

When you know yourself, when you realize your true identity, the meaning of life does not come to you in the form of a conceptual answer to a question. It is not an answer in your mind. It is you. The presence, fullness, and intrinsic preciousness is directly experienced; it is not in reference to anything else. It is complete autonomy; only the experience itself can give a taste of this satisfaction. This experience of self-realization is the answer, in the sense that it ends the drive. It is true absence of seeking.

When we want to explore our true identity, we have to allow ourselves to refrain from using our various roles, activities, ideals, and images to fill our sense of emptiness. Then we can observe whether any of these things actually satisfies our deep need for meaning. If you observe yourself, you will probably discover that you have become disappointed in one thing after another. You will see that you are disappointed in your career, the relationship with your lover or spouse, your own mind, everything. You're disappointed because they don't do what you hoped they would do for you. You are expecting the wrong thing from each area of your life that disappoints you. There is one disappointment after another until you allow yourself to fall into the great chasm, the great split. You need to allow yourself to exist in that vast emptiness. We must go through this non-existence. There is no other way.

To become unified, we must go through the split in us, which is the same thing as the chasm. We cannot go over it or avoid it. We must allow ourselves to experience the chasm. We have to allow ourselves to feel the insignificance completely, without defending against it.

When you recognize the feeling of being fake without trying to change it, and when you do not defend against it, you will feel complete nothingness, worthlessness, complete lack of support, complete helplessness. It is not that our process creates it; no, we have to go through it because it is there. This hole is there in our depths, and we are constantly avoiding it. When we allow ourselves to experience it, we might learn that emptiness is nothing, only peacefulness, and that the chasm is nothing but a boundless peace. It is an emptiness, and it doesn't have a selfhood, but it is not as scary as we imagine. One reason we are so frightened of it is that it is experienced as a kind of death. Even though you feel terrified of death before it happens, when you experience death, you will see that death is a resting place, a transition.

But we confront it only when we must; no one confronts this issue at his leisure. Nobody explores it out of a little curiosity. No, we have to confront this chasm from dire necessity, when we know that life is not worth it all. That's when you totally let go to the experience and know the meaning of death. And when you know the meaning of death, you know the meaning of life. This death is actually the death of the cork we talked about; it's the absence of all the attempts to fill the hole, all the fantasies of what will really do it for you. If you allow this letting go to happen, then there will be the beginning of a rebirth. You will begin to discover who you are intrinsically, your significance, and the point to your life. Existence and preciousness now are not caused in any way. We are the causeless reality which we have to experience ourselves. Just being oneself, life has meaning. You will be the meaning. Your true preciousness is the meaning.

It is not that when you go through the emptiness you'll feel "Oh, now I have a true self." The perspective of having something is the perspective of the separate self, the personality. So it is not that you are a little brilliant entity and you have love, compassion, beauty; no, the whole shift happens because the true identity is the identity with all Essence, with all of reality. This very moment, not related to past or future, is the center, and from there you can see that you are nothing but grace. Not only does life have meaning, but it is a grace, as if the heavens opened and poured grace into you.

You will see that your very nature is that grace, pure, un-originated preciousness, which you don't see by looking but by being. There is no sense of separateness between the looking and the being; they are one act. To be yourself means you are Essence, you are Being, you are the significance, you are the meaning.

We have seen that we are always looking for the preciousness that was lost, thinking we can get it from the outside. But it is the innermost. It is so private, so deep, so inner, that there is nothing more inner than this. Who you are is so inner, so private, so precious, that when it is experienced at its depth it is felt as an absolute sacredness.

To really be oneself is to eliminate the chasm, to unify the two sides of oneself, to fully become one. It is not as if you are someone who has a body, someone who does this or that, someone who has an Essence. You *are* it! You are the whole thing.

Meaning is not something we can get to with our minds; it is not an answer found in the mind. It is not an ideal or an image we're fulfilling. It is not a result of anything. It is just falling into one's nature.

To be able to simply fall into one's nature, is, however, not easy. It is the most difficult thing there is. It takes perseverance, patience, sincerity, and compassion for oneself. And it may take a long time.

FIVE

Essence and the Ego Ideal

A.H. Almaas: Today it's your turn to ask questions. Student: I'm confused about goals and expectations. Some people say that you have to have goals to live your life, and other people say that you can get caught up in goals and live too much in the future, planning and expecting things. Is having goals a mistake, or does it fit in some way?

AH: Generally speaking, there are two ways of living with regard to goals. One of them is being motivated by pursuing certain goals; this is the usual way people live in our society. The goals can be anything—to become a basketball star, a musician, or President; or to become rich, secure, famous, enlightened, or whatever. Generally, people cannot live without goals, because without goals, they feel aimless and lacking in meaning or significance in their lives. Without goals they often feel they have no orientation, and most individuals cannot tolerate this feeling.

People often decide on certain goals very early in childhood. These goals are largely determined by what we call the "ego ideal." For the normal personality, the ultimate goal is the realization of the ego ideal—to become your ideal, whatever it might be.

The problem is that when you are trying to reach a goal, you are separating yourself from your present reality. You are not living in the present, and you are rejecting who you are at the moment.

You set goals to accomplish certain things or to be a certain way because you believe that the way things are and the way you are at the present time are not good enough, and won't get you what you want. You also think that having no goals would mean that you would be bored or lazy or half-dead, or that there's something wrong with you.

Having goals in this way is one way to live your life. A second way is to live in the present, to be who you are at the moment, as a completeness and a fullness. This means actualizing who you are. At any moment you are who you are, and there is no need to be anything or to go anywhere. It is because you are not who you are that you want to be something, and you create all these goals and aims. Because who you are is missing, you have no true direction; your life feels meaningless, insignificant, with no value and no orientation. You attempt to fill this deficiency with goals and ideals and aims in order to create a sense of significance, meaning, fullness, importance, orientation, direction. However, when you let yourself be who you are instead of trying to be something different, you experience everything in your life as significant and important without even thinking of things as significant and important, by virtue of just being, just living.

This kind of living does not exclude goals. A person living in the present can have goals, but the goals are not to be something; the goals are an expression and the result of who the person is at the moment. The person is already fulfilled, and that fulfillment can then manifest as certain goals.

The difference is like that between a writer who wants to publish a book to be famous and a writer who wants to publish a book so his knowledge can benefit others. The latter has the same goal, but that goal is not intended to get him anything. He doesn't need fame or recognition from the outside. The goal comes out of an overflowing, an abundance that wants to give from itself.

From this perspective, life can be lived as an overflowing, as a spontaneous movement from the now, in which the goal is not something to arrive at. The goal is accomplished without effort; it's a natural flow. Because there's a fullness, the goal manifests as a spontaneous and natural movement from that fullness. Things just seem to flow in a certain direction. The person who isn't living according to goals doesn't need to organize himself rigidly and be strict about how this or that will happen. He doesn't really have to plan much. What happens is a product of his natural process, not a planned activity.

For instance, the way this group started and the way it has expanded has not been according to a plan. I had no plan for how it would happen. The Work kept changing and moving, and at some point, the movement necessitated a certain direction. It continues to unfold, and I have no idea where it will go.

We see that ultimately the true life is an aimless life; aimless not in the sense that it's just drifting along with no significance, but that it is rooted in reality. It is so rooted in reality that it doesn't need an aim. It has already attained the aim of all aims.

This perspective can help you to see that you need to question your goals and what you want from them. Are you wasting your life trying to achieve a goal that is a compensation for a deficiency you feel? Or is your goal an expression of who you are? Where do these goals come from? Where did you get them? Why is it you want so much to be an artist? Is it because your grandmother who liked you and gave you cookies and milk after school every afternoon happened to paint on Sundays? Or is there something inside you that wants to paint, regardless of what happens?

S: I have a question about the ego ideal. It seems as though your ego ideal, what you're trying to achieve, is also the characteristic you really wish your parents had seen in you and that you want others now to see in you. It feels like the most important part of who you think you are. I'm wondering if the ego ideal is a real part of oneself.

AH: It is, but not exactly. It is connected with ideals and goals. Heinz Kohut, the founder of Self Psychology, defined the self in terms of ideals and goals. This is true for the ego self, but not for the essential self.

As the ego self, we don't believe that we can be loved just for the mere fact of being who we are, independent of our various qualities. One of our deepest desires is to be seen and loved not because we're helpful or original or wonderful in some way, but simply for who we are. And we feel hopeless that this will happen. We feel that having certain qualities is what's going to get us the acknowledgment and admiration we want. We idealize one of these qualities in particular, and this is the ego ideal. We believe the ego ideal is the best part of us, and we want others to see this in us.

Sometimes, however, instead of idealizing a particular quality, some people idealize who they truly are, and make the essential self into an ego ideal. People who idealize being authentic, original and spontaneous, for instance, are actually idealizing qualities of who they truly are. However, this idealization does not mean that they are actually being who they truly are. An idealization is always a distortion of one's reality.

Usually, though, a person idealizes a certain quality that he has, and wants to be admired, loved, recognized, and respected for that quality. But as I've said, deeper than this wish is the desire for who he simply is, regardless of what he does, to be seen as precious. And there is a deep despair because who he is is not seen as precious, and the ego ideal is one of the compensations for this.

S: Where does the desire to be seen come from?

AH: When a child is between one and three years old, being seen is a developmental necessity. It's not a desire on the child's part; it's actually a necessity for full growth. For a child to be who he is, he needs to be seen and recognized for who he is. This admiration and recognition helps him to know himself. If this doesn't happen, the child will not experience who he truly is.

This lack of recognition is a universal occurrence. What parents really recognize their child? Your parents have to first know who they are in order to recognize who you are—the you that is really you regardless of what you do, the you that is your preciousness as a being.

Parents generally have their own ideals and goals, and they want their child to live according to these ideas. They don't say, "Oh, let's find out what this baby's all about." Parents usually have an idea of what kind of person they're going to raise before the baby is even conceived. The mother might already be thinking, "Well, when he grows up I want him to be a doctor." And if the baby is a girl, she grows up wishing she were a boy and wanting to be a doctor.

This matter is even more complex and subtle. Not only do we need to be seen in order to be who we truly are, but when we are not seen, we can only conclude that who we are is not good enough.

What is the child going to think? She believes her parents know everything, that they're wonderful and perfect. Then the parents don't see who she is. If you were a child, what would you conclude? Who you are must not be good enough; you must be flawed. What do you do then? You reject yourself. You reject yourself because you feel they reject you. The moment you reject who you are, there's a hole left, and you don't see yourself any more.

S: Do we reject all of ourselves, or is there a part that continues? Is that the key to survival for each of us?

AH: This is a complex question. A person usually rejects who he is, but that does not mean he rejects all his qualities and capacities. He rejects the most central part of himself, which has to do with the identity of his being. So part of his being might be there but he doesn't identify with it. He feels, "I have love," but he doesn't feel the love is *him*. He might still have intelligence but he doesn't feel, "I am intelligence." The identity with the quality is rejected.

S: Is there a particular aspect of Essence that tends to be more present in each person from the very start, or does the ego ideal make one aspect more significant?

AH: Usually the quality that is most present is the one that constitutes the ego ideal, because that aspect was a strength the person had from the beginning, which probably got some support or recognition from the parents, even if it was distorted. For instance, the aspect a person idealizes could be compassion. Since childhood, he has had a kind of compassion that is more obvious than other qualities. The parents might see this and reward the child for being helpful, for giving himself up for his parents. The child becomes very considerate and sympathetic, a peacemaker. However, the actual aspect of compassion is also there, along with the false qualities of self-sacrifice which the parents have supported. The two combined make the ego ideal.

S: Between the ego ideal and the identity—who we really are—what is there? Is there a space, a void, a kind of disconnectedness?

AH: There is an abyss. In the theory of holes in the Diamond Approach, you first become aware of how you try to fill the lack of an essential aspect, then you see a hole, an emptiness, where the aspect is missing. If you explore this, the essential aspect that was blocked will begin to arise.

However, when you begin to see through the ego ideal, you see something different. You see a hole, and in the middle of the hole there's another essential aspect. For instance, if you idealize who you truly are, you will experience a certain hole, and in the middle of the hole is the personal essence. You don't see just the hole. A person can try to fill the hole with another part of himself, but this doesn't work, because the hole is an absence of a particular aspect. If the hole is the hole of the true self and you're trying to fill it with compassion, it won't work.

S: What happens to the center that's in the middle of the hole?

AH: You're not aware of it. It's blocked. The hole means that aspect is cut off, repressed. The result is a deficiency, a hole, and the person attempts to compensate for the hole with the ideal.

It's as if you're trying to walk, and instead of using legs, you're trying to use your eyes. How can that work? It can't work! But the eyes are something real; you do have eyes.

If you try to use your mind instead of your heart, you can only go so far. You can think in your mind about your feelings, but that's not the same thing as actually feeling your feelings. But your mind is something real. That's what it means to compensate for something. You use one thing to compensate for the absence of something else.

The ego ideal is a compensation for a certain loss. Goals are also a compensation, an attempt to fill a certain hole.

Society is primarily structured around these compensations. Everybody has goals and ideals and plans, and they're all compensations for the absence of the essential self. Everyone is living his life as a compensation.

That is why in time, when you become more in tune with yourself and know yourself better, the roles you perform in your life, along with your capacities, become different. Ultimately, your gift to the world is being who you are. It is both your gift and your fulfillment. You can then exercise your capacities and abilities, attaining pleasure, joy, and fulfillment in your life.

S: What is the relationship of what you are saying to "being in the world but not of it"?

AH: That is what I'm talking about. To use capacities and qualities to attain fulfillment can mean being in the world but not of it. This means living among people and doing what everyone does, but in your center you are in a different place. The motives you have are different from the motives of most people. You might appear to be like everyone else, but you're not really. Inside, you are a different kind of creature.

S: I'm wondering about something I heard—that it's useless, even counter-productive, to work on yourself.

AH: That's true. When you get to subtle levels, you see that the ultimate paradoxes in your work are vicious cycles. This is why some people say it's better not to do anything about yourself and forget about it. To work on yourself is, at a certain point, to split off from yourself. What does working on yourself mean? It's artificial. You're trying to do something to "be" yourself. How can you do something to become who you already are?

At the beginning, from the perspective of the superego, you want to become better. But what is "better"? Basically, you believe that to become "better" means actualizing your ego ideal. You just take the Work and fit it with your ego ideal. After a while, when you see through this motivation, you might not use the Work for superego reasons. You might genuinely want to be yourself. But even that falls short, because there's nothing you can really do to be yourself. How can you try to be who you already are? You can only try to be who you are by separating yourself from who you are. That is what most people do all their lives. You have to go through this all the way and frustrate the hell out of yourself before you can see that it doesn't really work. The Work speeds up the process. The clearer it becomes, the more you really see you cannot try to become who you are. At some point you give up trying to be who you are. When you give up trying to be who you are, you just are.

Some people hear me say this and they think, "Okay, there's no point in doing the Work. I'll just go camping." But that isn't the answer. You have to come to the point at which you're one-hundred-percent convinced that nothing you try to do will give you yourself. If you say, "No, I'll go camping—maybe that will get me what I want," you're still trying. In fact, you're avoiding not trying.

The Work is needed. It's needed to expose many things until a certain time comes when the Work becomes a barrier; when you see that the Work, not just this work, but any work you do on yourself, just gets in the way. The moment you try to do something to work on yourself, you're separating from yourself. But you have to get to the point where you understand this completely before you can let go of trying. When you are convinced of the futility of what you're trying to do on all levels, then you let go. This will mean ultimate surrender. Before this happens, you're going to try, and you might as well try that within the perspective of the Work.

S: You talk about meditation from the standpoint of being present. I don't know whether I'm just beginning to be aware that I was not present before, or I'm really having trouble being present.

AH: It could be either, depending on whether there are certain things arising that are making it difficult for you to be present.

The best attitude for doing the meditation is to forget about results. Forget about what will happen when you do the meditation—just do it. When you meditate, you might not feel your presence, but that is fine. Just the doing of it is what's needed. Sometimes you will feel present, sometimes you won't. Sometimes you'll feel wonderful, sometimes you'll feel miserable. These factors do not determine the value of meditation. What determines the value of meditation is that you do the meditation. If you really do it, in time you'll become present mainly because you will not go along with the judgments and the preferences of the ego. You tell yourself that for twenty minutes a day, whatever your ego says, you're going to do it. This attitude by itself brings the true will, which brings true presence and detachment from the ego. The meditation is oriented toward presence.

The connection between just doing it and the issue of presence is very subtle. What stops us from being present are our beliefs and going along with the attitudes of the mind or the ego. That's really the main barrier. It is possible to be more present by putting out effort, by focusing on certain things. The meditation does both: it requires a certain effort, and there is actual work on the ego through the perseverance.

It's necessary at first to make the effort to be more present. But ultimately you need to be present without effort, to just let yourself be. Ultimately, presence is the same thing as Being, which does not involve trying to accomplish anything. To some extent, you can be present by trying to be present, but this is not being freely present. You can use your will and your effort to focus—and it's true, you are more present, but as long as you have to make that effort, you're not present naturally.

S: When we talked about the ego ideal the last time we met, it seemed like we got a pretty clear idea of what our ego ideals are. But talking about the essential aspect that permeates the ego ideal is less clear. I'm not sure what that aspect is in myself.

AH: It's not a simple thing to recognize one's ego ideal or to recognize the essential aspect that is part of it. I'm sure many people felt that they saw their ego ideal right away. That doesn't mean their perception was accurate. A person might say, "Oh that's my ego ideal," but the ego ideal has a subtle way of hiding.

You're dealing with something that runs your life, and part of what gives the ego ideal power is that it's not clearly recognized. It manifests in all kinds of goals and preferences, and to see it clearly, exactly, will precipitate a certain kind of experience.

To recognize the essential aspect, you must first of all accurately recognize your ego ideal. Second, you have to have some experience of the essential aspect in order to isolate it. Some people in the group have not had enough experience yet with essential aspects to be able to pinpoint theirs exactly. They confuse some essential aspects because they're similar. There may be other reasons for the difficulty, such as resistances and barriers against seeing these things. As I have said, really recognizing the ego ideal precipitates certain emotional experiences. If the person is unwilling to tolerate those emotional experiences, his process will be unclear and ambiguous. The exercises we do here are more difficult than they seem. They require clarity and precision and a deep knowingness of oneself.

S: I thought I really knew what my ego ideal was, but now I feel confused.

AH: You may know your ego ideal in a general way for years, and still not see how important it is. And the emotional connection around the ego ideal might not be apparent, because you do not yet have a certain precision.

There's a saying: The best place for a devil to hide is behind the altar. Here the altar is the ego ideal, which is what the ego hides behind.

S: Even if you identify the ego ideal, how do you come up with that permeating essential aspect?

AH: As I said, to be able to recognize the essential aspect, you need to know something about the essential aspect and you need to know to some extent how your childhood history shaped the ego ideal. This process requires a lot of self knowledge. If you haven't recognized the essential aspect, that's fine; it will become clear as you become clearer about yourself. The ego ideal, you must remember, is something you cherish dearly. You feel it is very close to your heart. You're not about to say, "Oh, it's just an ego ideal." You want to believe it completely; in a sense, you want to believe that it will get you to God. It's not easy to isolate it because of all your beliefs and attachments to it.

One way to recognize the ego ideal is to actually fulfill it. This happens once in a while. You actually achieve your ego ideal, and then you find it doesn't do what it's supposed to do. You finally attain the ideal, and nothing has changed. You're disappointed. "Now I've got what I've always dreamed of, but where is paradise? I thought that if I were really gorgeous, everybody would love me. Now I'm in the newspapers and on magazine covers and all that, and my mother still doesn't love me."

You generally don't question your ego ideal until you reach this point. Until then, you're basically trying to live up to it. You're not willing to look at or question the ego ideal before then, unless, of course, you come to someone who makes you think about it.

S: Once you give up and decide not to try to live up to your ego ideal anymore, then what?

AH: Some people have ego ideals that don't work. They're fifty or sixty years old, and it hasn't worked and they say, "Oh, I should work on myself now. I've heard about these Sufi schools, so maybe I should travel to the Middle East." So the person gives away his Cadillac and gets a knapsack and travels to Afghanistan looking for the Sufi Masters. Like many people who went to Afghanistan, he's told by the Sufi Masters to go back and study with such and such a person at such and such an address, and it turns out that this teacher was his next door neighbor. There really are stories like that.

If you have enough sincerity and have reached that point, you just need to let go. Let yourself sink into the experience and don't try to fill the void that results. If you learn to accept this void, then something fresh might happen. When you see through the ego ideal, you see it was filling a hole. You usually cannot tolerate the hole, and try to fill it with other things. But if you learn to accept the voidness, then there is the possibility of transformation.

When someone achieves the ego ideal and sees that it doesn't work, the attempts to fill the hole from then on are generally not effective. The person either tries to find another, similar ideal, or he simply modifies it. The ego ideal is always based on some kind of positivity—its aim is to give you a positive experience. It is a defense against a negative identity, a negative sense of self. There was a state of harmony that was lost, and the ego ideal is an attempt to regain that harmony. However, the loss of the state of harmony means the presence of negativity. The ego ideal is, in a sense, a way to deal with that negativity by retaining the hope for regaining a positive experience.

If a person sees through the ego ideal, he will begin to experience a negative state, which is the absence of the original harmony. He will have to deal with the negative part of the self that is angry and hateful, and will have to see his self-hatred and self-rejection.

In other words, you were in paradise and you were then thrown out of it into hell. You then try to build a certain ideal based on a hope of getting back to paradise, so you won't be suffering in hell. You have this fantasy in your mind while you're in hell, believing that if you work hard enough at being a certain way, you'll get back into paradise. The moment you give up that hope, you find out you really are in hell, and you experience the depth of the negativity of self-hatred and self-rejection.

When you recognize the ego ideal, there will be all kinds of defenses against it. I'm not trying, by the way, to tell you what will happen in your process; we're just trying to understand the process. If you're trying to anticipate what will happen, you are already motivated by the ego ideal. You want a result; the result you have in mind can only be a product of your ego ideal. You're still caught in it, ensnared by it. The best approach is simply to understand it. Then you'll see what will happen. It will not happen exactly the same way for everyone.

The ego ideal is very tricky. Even when you sincerely feel that you want to be free from it, you have to ask yourself why you want to be free from it. You want to be free so that you can be in a state of harmony. But that's exactly what the ego ideal is trying to do! If you go about this process from the perspective of wanting to understand these issues in order to have a certain result, then you're still controlled by the ego ideal. How can you be free from it then?

You will see that the mental activity of your ego is incessantly trying to think, feel, and behave according to the ego ideal. For instance, if your ego ideal is to be original or authentic, then you'll find that you're incessantly trying to be yourself. You're incessantly trying to change things in yourself so you can be closer to your ego ideal of who you think you really are. The activity itself is idealized.

The person who idealizes love is always trying to be loving. He's constantly thinking about how to be more loving with this person or with that person in this situation and that situation. His thoughts and feelings and activities are all colored by that aspect. So the person never allows himself to actually be that aspect. This is a distortion of the real quality.

Another example is the person who idealizes knowing. He is always engaged in trying to know things; he believes that if he knows this or that, he'll be free. To this person, not knowing is hell; most of his activity in life is involved with knowing.

The person who idealizes competence is always interested in action, using power, doing things; the one who idealizes love is concerned with helping, being loving and good. There are people who idealize being a protector. Their activity always has to do with protecting and defending. They think that if they defend enough, if they are the perfect defender of Essence, then they'll actualize Essence. So all their activity, both internal and external, has that flavor to it. You can recognize the essential aspect of the ego ideal by seeing the flavor of all your activities and concerns. This flavor is present on all the personality levels, and on all the subtle levels. The only time it's not present is when you are truly yourself. At other times, there's always some activity going on that is meant to accomplish something.

Your activity depends on your ego ideal. If you idealize strength, for instance, it doesn't mean you're just trying to be strong; it could mean you're always trying to be perfect in strength. Everything that you do that is important has some concern about strength in it. You don't want to feel weak. You don't want to take weak action. You're always proving to yourself that you're strong.

S: While you were talking, I identified a lot with all of the examples you gave. Is it possible that I idealize more than one, or a group of them?

AH: It's possible that you're confused. The confusion is a cover-up to prevent you from seeing the essential aspect you idealize because there are difficulties about it. The moment you recognize it, you would begin to feel all kinds of things that you'd rather not feel.

It's important to remember that the idealization is experienced not only as an aim to accomplish, but also that the activities are always colored by that aim. You believe, in a very deep place, consciously and unconsciously, that if you just do a certain thing perfectly, it will get you what you want. You believe, for instance, that if you're perfectly loving, you'll get everything you ever wanted, everyone will love you, you'll be free, and you'll find paradise.

S: If a person wants to live a life of strength, and this is his ego ideal, the first thing his ego ideal would want is to be strong. Then is the essential aspect that permeates the ego ideal what's uncovered after he's recognized the ego ideal?

AH: Yes. You see, if the person has strength as the essential aspect, the ego ideal is not necessarily strength; it's more complex than that. The essential aspect is one element that colors a complex image.

For somebody who has strength as his essential aspect, the ego ideal might be taking radical action as an anarchist in order to change society using strength and power. He believes that he can change the world and bring about harmony through revolution. He wants to change the world by being strong in a politically aggressive way, by overthrowing the government. But another revolutionary might have a different ego ideal, and want to change the world by acquiring revolutionary knowledge, a new knowledge that no one has had and that could change the whole world. So although the ego ideal seems to be the same, the essential aspects hidden within it are different.

The ego ideal is a self-image, an ideal image of yourself that contains many qualities. But the central pillar is the essential aspect that you idealize. The ego ideal that is built around this central pillar is a complete image of yourself, which determines what kind of person you will be, what kind of thoughts you will have, what kind of action you will take, what kind of life you will live, what kind of people you will be with.

S: Can your ego ideal be just to be?

AH: Yes, that's possible. "Just to be" could become your ego ideal. However, a person with that ego ideal probably grew up with parents who have some religious or spiritual background because the ego ideal has a lot to do with what your parents idealized. If you lived with Buddhist monks, you might have developed that ego ideal. But living in Western society, I doubt one would because being is not an ideal in this society. Generally speaking, action and movement and accomplishments are the ideals here. It's possible that one's ego ideal could be to be oneself, but that would be very unusual.

S: How does the idealization connect to the false pearl?

AH: What we call the false pearl, or the personality, is the result of living or trying to live according to the ego ideal. The false pearl is an overall description, whereas the ego ideal can be seen inside you. It is a certain structure that you can actually see floating around. The ego ideal is what I call the "dot." It is in juxtaposition to the true self—what I call the "point."

When you see your ego ideal on the level of subtle perception, you see a dark dot; and when you open it, you feel that you are an idea. You realize very distinctly that your ego ideal is really just an idea in your mind.

The false pearl, the personality, develops as you try to live according to the ego ideal. It's the activity itself, what you learned to do, what you have developed instead of your Being; it's what you have become. To put it very simply: the false pearl is what you have become by living or trying to live according to the ego ideal. .

S: Would you talk about the relationship between the self and the personal essence?

AH: Very good—the relationship between the self and the personal essence, or what we call the "point" and the "pearl." The false pearl is the personality which has developed according to the ego ideal. The personal essence, the personal beingness, on the other hand, which we call the Pearl Beyond Price, develops by living according to your essential self. This essential development can take place only when you are not separate from yourself.

When you are who you are, when you are just precisely yourself, you are your "point." Just that. This has nothing to do with any qualities, functions, capacities, and skills you may have. It has nothing to do with your status in the world, and nothing to do with living this life in a body or not in a body. It is your nature.

The Pearl Beyond Price is the connection between this genuine center and all the capacities, skills, and understanding that are a part of your growth as a human being. It allows your capacities, functions and accomplishments to develop in a genuine way as an outgrowth of your spontaneous unfoldment. It is the result of living in the moment, living in a way that is true to who you are. This is your genuine personal life, your own development, your own growth. The pearl is the actualized individuation of your Soul.

So the personal essence is connected with your unique function, your unique work in this life. To actualize your particular unique work in this life means to be your personal essence. It is the essence of all that you have developed and integrated in your soul as you live a real life.

Everyone is born with the true self, with the point. Although we feel that the point is unique in each of us, the quality of the point is universal. Then how do people become so different in their personal lives? This is due to the particular development of their personal essence.

Your unique contribution, your unique personal actualization of your self, your unique understanding, your unique work, and your unique style of life all have to do with the personal essence. The personal essence is the person, actualized in his or her life, while the essential self—the point—is beyond this life and, in a sense, does not need a body. It is always the same; it never changes.

The personal essence, the Pearl Beyond Price, however, is a development; it is something that develops out of the Soul when its center is the true self in this life. It is your actualization of your beingness here. When you experience yourself as your beingness, as your personal essence, you feel that you've accomplished yourself—not just yourself in the sense of knowing who you truly are, but by knowing who you truly are you start growing and developing your potential. This is the personal essence—personal, with a sense of beingness. The essential self is the experience of "I"; the personal essence is "I am"—not only my identity and my sense of who I am, but myself as a person, here in the world. That being has many skills and capacities, plus wisdom, understanding, and a certain style of life. The true self can be seen as the source, as the inner God, and the personal essence can be seen as the product or the Son of God. In Christian terminology the true self is the Holy Spirit, and the pearl is the Son. The true self is beyond time and space, but the personal essence is in time and space as embodied Being. They're two parts of an identity that fit together.

S: Is it possible to have the pearl as the essential aspect that is your ego ideal?

AH: Yes. A person can idealize the personal essence. That person will idealize personal relationships, personal things, and being personal. The person is not interested in a universal, objective perspective. There will be an issue about being efficient, and about being a person who is unique in a personal way.

When you recognize your ego ideal and also recognize the essential aspect in it, what I call your particular "channel" opens. Your channel has levels of the essential quality which you don't recognize immediately; these levels manifest as part of a process. For instance, if a person idealizes strength, there are many qualities in the strength. Ultimately, it becomes the "red channel," which manifests as strength and power, and then as a sense of vitality and expansion. This develops into a lustiness, and as the red energy expands, it becomes passionate love. Passion is idealized. As this expands, there is an idealization of beauty. The red channel is the channel of beauty. You're not only powerful and expansive, you see and appreciate beauty— a glamorous kind of beauty—a beauty full of vitality and colors.

When you recognize the ego ideal, instead of having something to accomplish, you then have a special contribution that is an outflow of who you are. This can happen only by exposing the ego ideal, not by living according to it.

S: Some people seem to attain their ego ideal, but it doesn't necessarily make them feel fulfilled, so they try something else. Can we change the ego ideal if it doesn't get us what we want? Or do we have to let go of it?

AH: You do not change the ego ideal. It can be modified—but it still stays very much the same. Remember that I said the ego ideal is not only an attempt to regain a positive state, but it is also a way to defend against a negative state. As long as a person needs to defend against this negative state, he or she will just modify it. Otherwise the person will have to deal with that state of disillusionment and negativity and emptiness.

S: And to the extent that we can stop worrying and let go of trying to avoid that negative state of not feeling significant, recognized, respected, or loved enough, that would free us up to be.

AH: Yes. That's what happens. However, it's tricky because our interest in being free is a subtle barrier. It's true that being free will happen, but if that is what you are trying to achieve, you are still motivated by your ego ideal. So again, you need dedication to the truth.

When we see that the ego ideal doesn't get us what we want, we usually engage in feverish activity to seek other kinds of ideals. We feel panic and worry, and try to find something to replace the lost ego ideal. It's as if we've been hanging from a secure rope, and the rope gets cut, and we must grab for anything nearby to hold onto—a twig, anything! Panic! Very few people say, "Whew," and let themselves fall.

S: It seems that another alternative would be negotiation. For instance, I might accept climbing fewer, less steep mountains more slowly as a changed ego ideal, and say, "Okay, I can do this, and this is enough to make me feel good about myself"—and spend more time smelling the daisies.

AH: That's what psychotherapy attempts to do—make the ego ideal more realistic. The person becomes more realistic about his ideals and more adjusted, which can be an improvement. But this is not the resolution.

The ego ideal is connected to the grandiose self, but it is not the same thing. It is a less radical defense than the grandiose self. A person who depends on the grandiose self is someone who hasn't got much of an ego ideal. Normal people have an ego ideal. More narcissistic people have a grandiose self. The grandiose self believes, "I am such and such a way." This is less realistic than someone who has an ego ideal and believes, "I'm going to become that way."

According to depth psychology, the person who has developed an ego ideal is considered normal. A narcissist didn't have a chance to develop an ego ideal, and developed the defense of grandiosity, which is a much flimsier defense than the ego ideal. The ego ideal is more tenacious, deeper, more entrenched; it permeates the fabric of the personality.

Although the ego ideal is a good indication of normality, some people have more extreme ego ideals than others, and the more adjusted the person is, the more realistic is the ego ideal. For instance, a person might want to be all-knowing, to know everything there is to know. Another person might want to be a professor of philosophy. Both have to do with knowing, but becoming a professor of philosophy is actually possible. You can go to a university, get a degree, and become a professor who knows a great deal. This is a much more realistic ideal than wanting to be all-knowing.

S: Would you say that very unrealistic ego ideals break down more quickly?

AH: Yes. They have a tendency to break down because reality doesn't support them.

S: In other words, if you want to believe you're the king of the mountain, other people have to agree that you're the king of the mountain, over and over.

AH: Yes. Either that, or you pretend you don't hear people when they challenge your ego ideal. Someone tells you you're a little schmuck and you interpret it by saying that person is afraid of seeing that you are the king and is afraid of your power. So basically, you deny what others tell you, and you put them down. The grandiose self will tend to uphold itself by devaluing other people and refusing to see the reality around them.

S: It sounds like there's not much room in the grandiose self for opposing ideas.

AH: No. There's no room for reality and no room for other people's perspectives. It's a very rigid position. The grandiose self is very rigid, very brittle, and that rigidity makes it vulnerable.

Grandiosity is mainly a defense against deep hurt and vulnerability. This is the same hurt and vulnerability that the ego ideal hides, which is the hurt of the absence of self and value.

One way people become grandiose is having inadequate external guidance in childhood. To survive they had to believe they knew who they were and what to do, because they had no support from the outside. This means that breaking through the grandiosity will bring out the insecurity of having no support, the sense that there is nothing there to help.

S: Is the grandiose self associated more with particular fixations on the enneagram than with others?

AH: No. All fixations can have a grandiose self. Neither the ego ideal nor the grandiose self are particular to any fixation, although the particular quality that is idealized is associated with the fixation. In this society, a person acting from a grandiose self is usually seen as maladjusted, although the person himself would not agree with this. A person with an ideal self is seen as adjusted, since most people have ideals and goals.

S: Can you have an ego ideal and a grandiose self?

AH: Yes. Everyone has both to some extent. One of them is a sign of normality, the other a sign of vulnerability.

S: I've been trying to find a way to be free from my ego ideal, so I keep trying to propose certain possibilities. I asked about the possibility of negotiation, but you told me that's what psychotherapists used—you modify the ego ideal and make it a little more realistic, and then you have more time to smell the daisies. But that isn't the resolution, and it doesn't bring about freedom—even though you could probably live pretty comfortably with it.

AH: That's what most people do.

S: I also asked about letting go of the ideal as a way to achieve freedom, and you pointed out that this is a trap. So I'm wondering if you could suggest a constructive stance that would point me toward freedom.

AH: Very good. I have a suggestion: Look at what the motivating force is behind the desire to find an alternative.

S: Sounds like I'll have to look at more stuff!

AH: Most likely.

SIX

Disidentification and Involvement

Student: Could you discuss what it takes to disidentify from something?

A.H. Almaas: To be able to disidentify, to turn away from a certain experience, a certain self-image, your identity needs to be at a deeper level than the self-image at that moment. You cannot disidentify from something if you are identified with something that is more superficial than what you're intending to disidentify from. So if you are identified with a certain self-image and then some feeling arises and you find yourself unable to turn away from it, it might be because it is at a deeper level than you are operating at the moment. If it is deeper than you are, then you cannot disidentify. You need first to dive. And the diving is what will bring in the perception, the awareness and the understanding of the deeper level. Then it is possible to turn away.

Many people teach a practice of simply turning away from whatever happens. Some traditions talk about such a practice, but not everyone can do it. It is not possible to turn away from something if you are unconsciously identified with it. It's not possible, because you believe you *are* it, in a way that is deeper than your awareness at that moment. It is your ground. You cannot disidentify from your ground. First you have to become aware of it, understand it; then your awareness will be deeper than it. Then it is possible to turn away from it. So turning away from something is always turning away from something you have seen and understood. Turning away means not indulging in something you understand. However, if it is not a matter of indulgence, if it's something you actually don't understand, and if you are unconsciously identified with it, how can you turn away? There is no way.

What's needed then is an immersion experience—allowing whatever that experience is and becoming involved in it as completely as possible, in order to understand it. Notice in your experience of understanding yourself, part of the process is this immersion, is an involvement with the experience, whether it is a belief, an emotion, a contraction in the body, a sense of frustration, a sense of attachment to something—whatever is there is experienced completely, without trying to get rid of it. When there is a complete involvement with what is there in you, then after a while an understanding arises. Without involvement, the understanding will not arise.

For the process of understanding to happen, three elements need to be there at the same time. The element of disidentification is one of them, involvement is another. The third element is the quality of allowing. These elements can be there when there is harmony among the three centers—

the belly center, the chest center, and the head center. When there is this harmony, it is possible to experience fully, to allow, and to disidentify.

Now, what do I mean by these three elements? Each center contributes to the process of understanding. If the head center is functioning correctly, it means that space or emptiness is allowed. What is the significance of space and emptiness? Space and emptiness make possible the quality of allowing. When there is space in the mind, there is no self-image. You're not trying to stick to something in particular. You're not trying to go somewhere. The mind is allowing whatever is there to be there. So the head center's participation or contribution is space, which is an allowing, a welcoming in a sense—space for things to happen without rejection, without trying to hold on. You become complete allowing.

The heart center's contribution has to do with its central quality, which is the personal essence. The contribution of the personal essence is the diving movement, the actual living of the experience. You not only allow it, you're in the midst of it, you're one with it. You're really it, you let it happen, you feel it fully, you sense it fully, you experience it fully, right? That's the contribution of the heart center.

The belly center has its contribution, which is represented by the self, the essential self. The contribution of the essential self is the disidentification, the turning away. When you are truly functioning in the belly, you are completely present, and being completely present, you are being yourself. So you are not identified with the usual activity of trying to get somewhere else.

I am not implying that space is always in the head, the pearl in the heart, and the essential self in the belly. Centers lose their importance after a while in terms of locations of essential aspects. What I mean is that when space is functioning as allowing, it activates the head center; when the pearl is functioning as involvement, it is usually in the heart center; and when the essential self is functioning as disidentification, it is usually in the belly, in the Hara center.

So when these centers are functioning, allowing, involvement, and disidentification, are there all at the same time. The mind has space in which to allow whatever is happening; the heart is deeply involved, allowing you to dive, to expand into the experience; and the presence in the belly allows the identity to be there in the moment, not involved with images and ideas about past and future.

When these centers are functioning in harmony, then there is the force of understanding, which allows one to turn away from something. But you cannot have only one of them functioning and have the process of understanding run smoothly. You need the three elements there in equilibrium.

So just to disidentify is not enough. You cannot completely disidentify unless you're completely involved. If you disidentify the moment the experience arises, you don't even fully experience it. How can you disidentify if you don't allow it to happen? How can you disidentify if you don't know it completely?

Now someone who happens to be the true self all the time will tell people, whatever happens, just turn away from it. This person can do it because his identity is at the deepest level. You see? And that person who's always the true self can turn away from something because his identity is the deepest identity. But others cannot do that. Who is going to turn away? If you are identified with something in you, what does it mean to turn away? Who's going to turn away? Who's going to disidentify? We cannot disidentify from some mental content if we are unconsciously identified with a self-image that underlies this content.

S: I have an image of when I was my true self and I try to remember myself.

AH: The danger of this is that if you're operating from an image of what you saw yourself to be, even if it was the true self, then you're not allowing the experience that is here. There is a rejection, you see? And the true self doesn't do that. The true self doesn't try to bring itself back by having an image of itself. Only the mind does that.

You discover in time that you cannot operate according to a self-image, even if the image is of a true experience of yourself. What happens at this moment could be completely different from what happened then. Right? Who's going to decide what's supposed to happen now? Of course, your experience will have to happen many times until you really learn that it's true that you can't do it that way. The person doesn't give up that easily. The person says, "Well, I'll try now ..." You'll try 3,000 times, at least, before you get really tired and say, "I can't do it, it doesn't really work that way. Just because it worked three years ago, doesn't mean it's going to work now."

S: I'm wondering how you tell the difference between indulging in something that's already understood, and the need to immerse yourself in it.

AH: You need to be sincere with yourself. If you're sincere with yourself, you'll think, "You know, this is something I have known, I've experienced it many times. Why am I doing this again?" If you're really sincere with yourself, you'll see there's something there you don't understand. If you don't understand, and if you're not holding yourself back, the diving will happen naturally.

S: On Friday I had a migraine headache and I got to the point of saying "I'm not the frustrating child and I'm not the frustrating world." I could see that I was still stuck in it—with the pain and all the rest. But I just kept saying that; then I experienced this total disorientation. We were waiting to go into a restaurant and I didn't know where I was, I didn't know who I was, I didn't know who the person I was with was, really. My mind couldn't think. It felt like the ground was pulled out from under me.

AH: So what's the question?

S: The question is, was my experience of being totally disoriented moving to a deeper level of my identity, or was it just part of the personality?

AH: Disorientation is always the result of the presence of space and the resistance against it. People get disoriented, they get dizzy. Space means an allowing or a change is starting to happen, but it is not complete; there is still a resistance against it. So, there is the experience of temporary disorientation.

Usually, the best thing to do is to let the disorientation happen. If you try to resist it, you're resisting space, because space is an allowing factor. Of course, to allow the disorientation you need to be in the right circumstances, not driving on the freeway. Although sometimes even that is possible if other parts of you are more present.

S: That relates to my question. The identification with negative patterns often happens to me in situations, for example, when I'm teaching class and it doesn't seem appropriate to dive and yet I can't disidentify in those situations.

AH: Why isn't it appropriate to dive?

S: Well, to dive is to go deeper into the experience, in which case I couldn't function ... I mean, I might cry! My attention should be on doing what's appropriate in the circumstance, teaching the class.

AH: Isn't it possible to split your attention into two—a small part dealing with the class and a larger part dealing with what's happening with you?

S: Well, what's happening with me in this situation is that I'm threatened by the class and feel like I can't deal with it.

AH: That is the time to deal with it.

S: I mean, I'm threatened by the class and not dealing with it.

AH: That's the time when you need to deal with the threat, with the feelings. You can't say that now isn't the right time. What's going to happen? When you learn to pay attention to yourself, you can be in external reality with a minimum of attention, really. It doesn't take much. You may find out that you can do it more than you think. Everyone does it to some degree. The more you pay attention to yourself, the more awareness you have, and the more you're able to do it. When I'm working with someone, usually only a small part of my attention is with them. I am present and pick up everything, but it doesn't mean all my attention is there.

S: As you were talking about the correct functioning of the three centers, I was aware that my three centers don't always function correctly. In the case of the diving, is it best to be aware of a center that's not functioning, put a lot of attention on it, and try to understand?

AH: No, it's not a matter of putting attention on any particular center. It's a certain attitude. In the head center, the correct attitude is to allow things to happen. In the heart center, the correct attitude is involvement, participation. In the belly center, the correct attitude is disidentification.

So the awareness itself is enough. If you're aware that you're not allowing, you might see why you're not allowing things to happen. If you're aware that you're not participating, then you might find out what the resistance is, what the block against the participation is.

Sometimes what blocks participation or immersion are prejudices against that particular identification. One example is thinking that you should be beyond that experience because you think you understand it. It might make sense to your mind that it's a certain way, but it is not a lived experience. Of course, the more you understand yourself, the more you understand those parts of you, the more the centers will develop, the more the appropriate attitudes will develop in you, and the more capacity for understanding you will have.

S: I usually associate the belly center with the quality of embodiment or becoming something. I'm a little confused about that, especially the word "disidentification."

AH: Yes, usually the belly center has to do with embodiment, with the capacity to sense oneself. However, the belly center is also the will center. In a sense, the ultimate function of the will is to surrender to what happens, surrender to the now. And surrender to the now means not to hold on to something. The true function of the will is complete surrender to what's happening without holding on. That is will. The essential self, like all essential aspects, can function in any of the subtle centers. When one is being the essential self its location is usually the heart center. However, when the essential self is functioning in relation to identifying or disidentifying from any content of experience, it becomes associated with the belly center. The essential self is more like a potential for experience, and it also manifests as a capacity for identification. One of the results of that capacity for identification is embodiment. Embodying something means you are identified with what's happening. An essential state is present. You are embodying it if you *are it*. The true self has the capacity to identify with something you are experiencing, but it doesn't have to. It has a choice; it has the freedom.

When you are the true self, you can become completely what is there—one hundred percent. If truth is present, you are truth—"I am truth." But the moment something else arises, you become that. There is no holding on.

S: How is that embodiment different from the heart involvement?

AH: Participation is not the same thing as embodiment. Participation means experiencing it, living it, feeling it. It's like contact with what's happening. Contact with what's happening is not the same thing as identity with what's happening. There's contact, friction, touching in the heart center.

Are there any further questions?

S: Is the sensation of pain an indicator of disidentification?

AH: The sensation of pain is an indicator that something is happening that's not supposed to be happening. Basically, pain is always an indication of danger. No? When your stomach is hurting you know something is not right. Maybe you have an ulcer. You don't say, "I should disidentify from my stomach." We know, of course, that pain can be distorted, so sometimes we need to disidentify from our attachment to a certain pain. But that is not the basic thing about pain.

S: On Friday I had an incredible headache, and it seemed that the joy center was closed down. When that intense pain happens, it becomes so intense, it seems like an indicator that I should disidentify.

AH: You have that pain in the head now?

S: Well, today during meditation, it centered in my hips. I identify with those areas and I was resisting space in that area. Why is that pain necessary for me to get to Being?

AH: The pain is not necessary for you to disidentify.

S: Why is it there then?

AH: Your body gets tense and pain results. And the pain is an indicator that that you need to look at the tension.

S: I view that pain as the resistance to a lot of my energy.

AH: That's probably true. The pain helped you see that there was a resistance. So that was its job. The pain indicates that something that was happening there was not supposed to happen, was not natural. And what was happening was the tension.

S: Is pain used in that way by most people?

AH: You don't use it, it happens by itself. When tension in the body gets to a certain level, there is pain in any living organism. So the body uses it as a signal. There's pain; the body screams. Something not right is happening. You pay attention. That's what pain is for—to get your attention.

So it's not as if you can disidentify and just forget about it. That's not a good idea. If there is pain, you need to look. What's there? Why is there pain? If it doesn't go away after a few days, even when you understand things, then you should go to a doctor. Maybe you cracked a vertebra or something. So it's better to be still and pay attention. When you're crossing a street and a car is coming, you don't say, "I should allow and participate in this experience." You use your common sense.

S: What are archetypes? My experience here is dealing with personality and then Essence. I'm wondering, if archetypes exist, are they an extension of the individual personality on a cultural level, or are they manifestations of Essence?

AH: It depends on what you mean by archetypes. I don't know which school you refer to when you use the word "archetype."

S: It's something closest to Jungian...

AH: If you're referring to Jungian archetypes, then, as far as I know, Jung said that archetypes are images that contain universal experiences. An archetype accommodates different people's experience of the same thing. For instance, there's the archetype of the mother. We can all experience ourselves as the mother, right? According to Jung, archetypes are images. Images can be filled with experience.

S: So it could be either essential experience or personality experience?

AH: It seems so from what he said—some of them are personality, some of them are essential. An archetype is a concept, you have to remember. There are no such things as archetypes that actually exist in reality. We can experience ourselves as the mother, but there is no such thing as something everyone could experience in the same way. Some people at some point are mothers. That's the reality. The archetype of the mother doesn't exist; it's an image, a concept. It is not a presence. But something like the true self is something that exists. It's not just a concept. Concepts are useful, but it is important to be clear about whether or not something really exists.

S: Last night someone asked a question about having a higher spiritual self. In light of that, what is spiritual guidance or the feeling of guidance? Is it an aspect of Essence, or is it something else?

AH: Guidance? Guidance is an aspect of Essence.

S: But it seems personified as someone else.

AH: Well, the mind sometimes does personify it as an image. But it isn't an image. It's a part of you.

S: Sometimes it has a sexual quality, a masculine quality.

AH: Your mind is creating images for you. It is possible to see the guide more objectively—it doesn't have to be anything, it doesn't look like a person. The images that your mind makes are modeled according to the physical body; essential aspects are not. They have their own reality.

S: When you answer me, who do you talk to?

AH: It changes according to the situation.

S: My heart asked the question...

AH: It depends first of all on who can listen, right? Sometimes it's a part of your mind, sometimes it's a part of your personality, sometimes it's what's real in you, sometimes it's all of them together. This is not something that I decide. It depends on the flow of what happens. It can change within an interaction. At one point perhaps I'm talking to your mind, and after a while I'm talking to something else because you've changed. The way Essence always functions is to communicate in a way that starts where the person is and goes deeper. It starts where you are and moves to the next level. A person can sometimes experience that as pressure. Some people experience pressure as if I'm pushing them to go somewhere. I'm not intentionally pushing; I naturally function that way. When I'm talking to someone, they are moving to the next level, whatever is deeper in their experience. So there is a pushing, but it's a pushing to be yourself; it corresponds to an internal push from your Being.

S: Yesterday you talked about how some people idealize autonomy. What is the relationship between autonomy and the true self? How can the idealization of autonomy keep you from seeing your true self?

AH: The quality of autonomy might be used to substitute for the true self, to compensate for its absence. But it's the issue of idealization that needs to be understood and not the autonomy itself. If a person is not his true self, he needs an idealized self. A person who never attained autonomy would always think he was a failure. Another person might achieve his idealization and then be disappointed to discover that it didn't do what he thought it would do. People can either respond with despair and depression, or they use the occasion to try to explore why it didn't give them what they wanted. People who can question in a very genuine way in such a situation can arrive at the true self.

The person who achieves his idealization may have a better chance at finding his real self if he doesn't despair, but actually learns true hopelessness. If he doesn't reach his idealization, he may still find the true self, but it may be difficult for him to believe that that's what he needs. If the idealization doesn't break down, it is possible to experience the true self, but not value and appreciate it. The idealization must be exposed. Sometimes it has to be seen by working on yourself, rather than through the life situation. You can uncover beliefs and hopes and dreams by working on yourself, rather than having to act them out in life.

S: So where is the change, the transformation? Don't we just continually try to upgrade our ideals in response to disappointment?

AH: A person might not see his idealization clearly. If it is unclear, then he might change it in this and that way. So it remains fuzzy. Sometimes we keep our ideals fuzzy to avoid the moment of truth, the moment of finding out that they don't satisfy us. We fear the despair that we are sure will follow when we see that what we really wanted doesn't satisfy us. Then you have to die in one way or another. That is why some people commit suicide when they seem to "have it all."

When your idealization is just a distant dream, there is still something to live for, and the idealization gives you hope. But from another point of view, that apparent zest for life is just a part of what is creating the deeper suffering.

We want to arrive at the place where there is no hope, yet no despair. This rarely occurs naturally in our life situations without the work of understanding.

S: The Work is tricky that way. We get involved in idealizing consciousness.

AH: Yes, but it works with that, too. You become more conscious, you realize Essence, your heart is open. And you discover that you're just as miserable as before. "What happened?! I was enlightened yesterday!" "What's this? I was God-realized, I was enlightened, and look at me now!" It's the same thing.

Ambition is ambition. And then you realize, even enlightenment doesn't do it. It's not it. It's not the point. The point is not to worry and be happy. There isn't really even a point to get to—it's just that the centers are functioning harmoniously.

In time you realize that as long as you live according to any ideal, as long as you try to actualize any ideal, there is suffering. And you learn this through the process of suffering more than anything else. If you suffer deeply and with understanding, you will mature, you'll be a ripe human being. A ripe human being is a human being who feels deeply that at the deepest level there is happiness and harmony, but who knows at the same time, that desiring happiness and harmony cuts him off from reality. Because he is mature and he knows this principle, he stops desiring. A mature human being knows that he wants happiness more than anything else, and he also knows that by wanting it, he will not get it; so he acts accordingly. Another person might know these things, but not be mature enough to act accordingly. Being mature means that your knowledge allows you to actually stop pursuing your fantasies. But it takes a lot of disappointments to allow that to happen.

S: If not having goals, or reaching goals, or having low goals and reaching them, helps us become enlightened, what do we teach our children about goals?

AH: Teach your children to simply like themselves, that's all. If your child learns to be himself, like himself, that's enough. What do you need goals for?

S: To be able to live, to earn money, to be able to support yourself...

AH: Who says you need goals to support yourself? If you like yourself, you'll know you need to do some work and make some money to be able to live. So you'll do it and be happy, but it won't be because you have a goal.

S: But the goal is to have enough money to be able...

AH: No, that's not the goal. The goal is to be yourself, if you can call that a goal. There's no need for goals. That's just how we usually think. But look at it—that attitude is the source of your problems. If you don't have a goal, you can just let yourself be in the now. It's only your mind thinking, "Oh, there's something I must achieve," that makes you discontented. A goal requires control, a lack of spontaneity, a lack of flow. If there is control, how can there be joy? It's not possible.

The moment you control yourself, your joy is shut off— no joy, no happiness. You may be angry at God for making it that way, but that's how it is.

S: Why?

AH: That is a case you have to take to God.

And everyone in this work will at some point have a bout with God. The ultimate conflict is with God.

S: So what do you do when you have to do something that you don't want to do? The only way to do it is to control yourself.

AH: If you really like yourself, then you will do what you have to do easily. You'll know that you have to do it. Why dislike it?

Suppose you need to eat some evening. You don't like cooking, there is no food prepared, the restaurants are closed, so you have to cook. If you really like yourself, you'll enjoy your cooking, since you have to do it anyway. Why say, "Oh, I don't like cooking"?

A person who really loves himself likes doing what he has to do. It doesn't matter what it is. The liking and the enjoyment have nothing to do with the external activity. It has to do with accepting yourself. So it doesn't matter what you do.

Do you think it makes a difference, whether I'm talking to you, watching TV, cooking, driving a car, or swimming? Does it make a difference in my joy? Why should it make a difference? If it makes any difference, it's conditioned behavior, a restriction. Your external activity should not make any difference at all to your happiness. If it does make a difference, you're obviously identified with something that is not you. When you see that it doesn't really make a difference, you won't always be anxious to get things over with, or anxious about what's going to happen. The tension and anxiety will not be there, because there is no reason for it.

S: Does it mean I don't like myself because I hate to go to the dentist?

AH: Yes.

S: There should be joy in that pain?

AH: What does the joy have to do with the pain or no pain? Joy is different from pleasure in the sense that joy has nothing to do with pain or pleasure. We think pleasure is happiness, but it's not happiness. Joy is happiness. Pleasure is opposed to pain; joy is not. It is possible to have pain and joy at the same time.

So why block your joy just because there's going to be some pain? I'm not saying that you should push yourself to be joyful, but if it is possible for it to be there, allow it. Joy has to do with openness in the moment, with not choosing one thing over another. When there is no prejudice about what should happen, there is joy. Joy is openness to experience. There is no striving. Joy is not the result of anything. If you are yourself, there is joy. If you are accepting and open to your experience, if you're being yourself, you're naturally joyful because *you* are the source of the joy.

S: Is there a difference between joy and ecstasy?

AH: Well, ecstasy is a word that's used for different kinds of feelings, sometimes joy, sometimes love, or intense pleasure, usually something intense. The experience of your true nature could be called ecstasy. If you experience Essence completely, it's ecstasy. Joy, ecstasy, and pleasure are only a few modes of experience for the true self. There are many others that most people don't appreciate.

There are joy, pleasure, peace, compassion, gratitude, fulfillment, love in various forms—passion, melting, and so on. There are strength, power, preciousness, value, depth, expansion, freshness, clarity, brilliance, and so on. All of these modalities of experience are very satisfying. The experience of harmony, or completeness, can make all desires disappear. Pure awareness can be extremely blissful. What is wrong with pure existence? Why think only of happiness and pleasure? Others can be just as satisfying, and even more profound. The deepest satisfactions don't come from what people call joy and pleasure.

SEVEN

Non-Waiting

When you are complete, there will be no waiting. You anticipate and wait only when you are not complete, only if you need something, believe you need something, or feel you want something. When you don't feel a need or desire for anything or for the absence of anything, then there is no waiting. There is only Being. To be complete is not the same as thinking or feeling that you've got everything, nor does it mean that you feel good or full. It doesn't mean that you're experiencing yourself as an essential state, like pleasure or will. It doesn't mean that you have what you've always wanted.

To be complete means that you are not pulled by anything and you cannot be pushed by anything. It's not as if there are two ways of being, and you have the better one if you're complete. It has nothing to do with having anything. If you feel complete because you have something, then obviously you have some needs that need filling in order for you to be complete.

To feel complete means to be, which means knowing yourself as the one who cannot but be complete. It is not as if you were once incomplete, and then you became complete. If that were so, it would mean that your old needs and desires were fulfilled and, as a result, you became complete. It doesn't work that way. To be complete means to realize that you have always been complete, that who you are is a completeness. And being complete has nothing to do with better or worse, pleasure or pain, gain or loss. It has nothing to do with anything; it is not in reference to anything.

So when you know yourself in this way, when you are complete, there is no waiting. Time is not experienced as waiting for something. If you're not anticipating, wanting or fearing anything, then there is no waiting. There is just Being; you just are. And that "is-ness," that Beingness, will not necessarily satisfy your mind in terms of what your mind thinks is good or not good, since as I said, it doesn't mean you feel fulfilled or satisfied, full of strength or compassion or any other aspect. It's not a matter of having any particular quality. As long as you believe that you need to have something particular in order to be complete, you are not yet complete.

To be complete means to be thoroughly serene, totally, completely in repose, so much in repose that pleasure and pain come and go, but are irrelevant, surface phenomena. To be complete means you are not interested in things being any particular way. If you're complete, why would you have an interest in anything? You're not interested in getting; you're not interested in giving. There is just no interest. You're not interested in pleasure; you're not interested in pain. You don't reject or oppose pain if it comes; you don't even prefer its absence. To be interested means to move out of your repose; it means you have a need, and therefore are not complete. Completeness is the absence or end of interest, in the sense of preference.

So being complete means being totally serene and unperturbable. You have no need to accomplish anything or achieve anything, even completeness. You're too complete to think or reflect on your completeness at all. You don't even need to know you're complete.

It is interesting that you experience either completeness or incompleteness. Your mind is either aware of one or aware of the other. There is nothing in between. You are yourself only when you are complete. When you are not complete, you are not yourself. If you need anything, absolutely anything, if you desire or fear anything, you are still not completely yourself. Of course, your body will have its basic biological needs, like food and shelter. You attend to these, but you are not dependent on comfort to be complete.

If you experience yourself as incomplete, you remain unaware of your innate completeness, and behave like someone who needs to be filled. The behavior of someone who is incomplete is easy to recognize: the person always acts as if he wants or needs something.

As long as there is an itch for something, you know you are not complete. If you experience interest in anything at all—an object, a person, an activity, or an idea—you know that, in that moment at least, you're not complete.

It will probably sound to your mind as if being complete would make for a totally uninteresting life. Such a state does not sound appealing or appetizing. Yet the mind will not be able to rest until there is completeness.

Being complete doesn't mean that you don't do anything, that you just hang out and vegetate. When you are complete, your actions can only be loving. When you're not experiencing the gap of incompleteness, there is no need and no fear, and then you are free to love. Love is a natural movement; it doesn't need a desire to motivate it. Loving action is the spontaneous arising out of that completeness. And from that, all else comes.

Being complete does not necessarily mean knowing anything. Completeness is independent of the mind. The mind typically functions out of a sense of incompleteness. Much of its activity occurs because you take yourself to be incomplete. Only once in a while is it needed for conscious, practical functioning, and most of this happens without our having to think about it.

The mind spends most of its time designing ways to fill needs, satisfy desires, and quell fears. Whether you are meditating, watching TV, or taking a bath, there is agitation of the mind arising out of your own sense of deficiency, of holes needing to be filled. Almost everything we are engaged in is an attempt to fill that sense of incompleteness.

So if who we actually are is a completeness, and we have always actually been complete, why do we experience ourselves as incomplete? One way to see it is that the experience of incompleteness is actually the experience of a distance from your completeness. To be incomplete means to be separated from your completeness. There is a split, a gap between what you think you are and who you actually are. This split, this chasm occurred for some reason at some point in your history.

You have abandoned yourself. You have become separated from your real self. You are taking the constructs of your mind to be you. The moment you take yourself to be anything in your mind, you are split from who you are, and you will experience insecurity, fear, and desire. The separation from your real self will bring wants and needs, the thoughts that accompany them, the feelings that accompany those, and the rest of the mess that most people call their lives.

Once this chasm develops, what you take yourself to be is always based on it. How you experience yourself most of the time is based not on completeness, but on the absence of it, on a gap. So it is understandable that you'll have all kinds of wants, needs, desires, thoughts, ideas, ambitions, plans, and so on. From the deficient perspective of incompleteness comes a feverish activity to accomplish, to fill, to acquire. The desire to acquire something—an object, person, emotion, more knowledge, experience, pleasure or Essence—is based upon this sense of incompleteness, which is itself based on an incorrect understanding of who you are.

Identifying with your desire will only perpetuate the chasm by strengthening a self-image that is split off from who you are. In other words, you will not become complete by acquiring something you haven't got or by fulfilling a desire; you can't reach completeness by trying to complete yourself. Who you take yourself to be, your sense of yourself as incomplete, can't be completed because its very nature is an incompleteness. The chasm is infinite and cannot be filled. You can resolve this issue only by realizing that you are split. Seeing this and not acting according to the split can bring freedom. You fall back into yourself and realize that you are complete, that who you truly are has always been complete, and has never lacked anything, that you cannot lack anything.

Having this perspective helps us to orient ourselves towards self-understanding and towards our work here. We cannot help continuing to desire, and even to continue to believe our desires. We cannot help thinking the thoughts of a person who is incomplete. However, if you allow the possibility that this may all be a wrong identification, a split from who you are, your orientation may change. You might believe less strongly in your desire and fears, and begin investigating them more. Instead of acting out your desire for love or approval, recognition, acknowledgement, pleasure, or fame—any desire—you can begin to observe the desire itself.

The perspective of completeness does not condemn pleasure. We're not saying that pleasure is bad. When you know yourself as complete, there will be an experience of pleasure, but it will not perturb you, will not force you from your center. Pleasure is there and so is pain. You are beyond both of them; they have nothing to do with you. The pleasure and pain are of your body and mind.

We can also see from this perspective that ultimately, the only thing that will work is being, is for you in time, to value Being, just being. This doesn't mean that you're Being and you're waiting for something. You're not sitting there meditating so that something will happen. The Being is it. If you're waiting for something, you're believing in the gap.

The action of meditation can be very simple. It is perceiving the process of becoming, with its wanting, desiring, pushing, and pulling. You can just be aware of all that, because it is not Being. The more you're aware of this movement of becoming and allow yourself the possibility that it is not working regardless of what it's moving towards, the more you can observe and experience the gap directly. And if you don't follow any movement, attitude, or reaction to it, you may find yourself to be complete.

So completeness does not come as a result of any action or effort, nor is it the end of a process. The personality, the construct of your mind with which you identify most of the time, is a movement of becoming, always wanting to be something, wanting to get something, wanting to become something, go somewhere, move toward something. It's an activity; it is not a stillness. If you become completely aware of this movement, then you're not engaged in it. And when you're not engaged in it, you are the completeness.

Everything we do here is designed to create space for that completeness to happen. Our work is not oriented towards acquiring anything, although for a long time it will appear that you are acquiring, developing, or learning something.

But that is only the perspective of the mind, the perspective of the one who is incomplete thinking that it's getting more and more completed. Ultimately, though, you will see that you're not acquiring or getting anything from anyone. Becoming and getting are not the point. If you conduct yourself as though they are, you'll be wrongly oriented; you'll be moving away from completeness.

We don't come here so that we will get somewhere. We don't meditate for a result. No, the practice is for the moment; the experience of completeness can happen at any moment. You just let yourself be, rather than being engaged in becoming and desiring.

Being complete is not a big deal: you don't suddenly get what you want, have all your dreams fulfilled, see that all of life is colorful and wonderful. It's not like that; it's beyond that. If you're happy about being in paradise, then you're taking yourself to be someone who needs paradise—you're incomplete.

You're something much simpler, much, much simpler than all the paradises and pleasures. You're also much fuller, though it's not a sense of fullness. When you're complete, even the experience of paradise comes and goes and the experience doesn't move you. You're not pulled, or pushed, you're not tickled. You're tickled only if you're incomplete.

Of course, you might experience all kinds of paradises and wonderful things. That's fine. Why not? The completeness doesn't have an opinion about that. It doesn't say no; it doesn't say yes. It is unperturbed. It is the center. It is a very simple, little thing, but without it, there is incompleteness and there is an endless search.

The life of the personality is created from the absence of that simple, little thing. Without it, any experience lacks something, regardless of how wonderful and sublime it is. But, when you are complete, everything is as it is. Your perception is not colored by the distortions of incompleteness.

You don't need it to be one way or another. You see it very simply. There's no big deal in it, nothing dramatic. Completeness is so simple that it is purity itself, a sense of freshness, fresh air, a clear breeze.

When you're complete, you can be; you can just be and not take any action whatsoever for a million years, and there's no waiting, no desire for things to change or not change. From this completeness arises the only action possible then, which is love. Love becomes the basis of one's life. It is abundance.

So the process of the Work becomes an exploration of the desires, fears, wants, gaps and holes, uncovering them one by one, so that in time you stop believing they are real or necessary. Most people live their lives believing that their desires, fears, and plans are real, and that they determine what's supposed to happen. And when fulfillment is not forthcoming, the result is disappointment and surprise.

Fulfillment, which is simply the absence of the lack of fulfillment, arises through denuding yourself, baring yourself, becoming more and more naked. It's a matter of letting go of the things you've been trying to fill yourself with, of shedding the unreal, until you're so simple that you're simplicity itself. Your mind can't even think about you. You're not complicated enough to think about you, to reflect on yourself in the way you've been used to. The mind doesn't know what to do about this simplicity. It can't categorize or analyze it.

People usually come to the Work feeling that they have a lot of gaps and holes it will help them fill. While the Work will not fill these gaps, it can show you that you're trying to work on something that is not you and thinking it is, that if you see rightly, you will see that you don't have gaps, you don't have holes.

It's not necessarily an easy process. The mind and personality have accumulated many inaccurate beliefs, preconceptions and presuppositions. You could say that the Work is a process of education or re-education, though not in the traditional sense, since it is a shedding, rather than an accumulation. You are learning to be simple, and that simplicity is the completeness.

A person who is not self-realized is a complex person. The person who knows him or herself truly is very simple; there's nothing there to understand and no complications. It's not as if they're so simple that it's easy to understand. They're so simple that there's nothing to understand. You just are, and that's it.

Student: How does completeness relate to awareness?

A.H. Almaas: Completeness is beyond awareness. It is just Being itself. You're complete without having to know that you're complete. From that Being comes awareness; it is the light of Being. Being itself is beyond mind, beyond knowledge, beyond awareness. If you allow yourself to be the awareness, you will become the completeness. The completeness is the awareness with the absence of desires. If you're not identified with the past as desires, then the awareness becomes completeness. It's not as if the completeness is not already there; it is there. But you're taking yourself to be something else. As I said, it's not something to reach. We miss it because it's something so simple, so already there. It is when there are no desires, needs and fears, or when you're just tired of them and rest, that you realize there is completeness. When you can see the desires, the fears, the pleasures and the pain, when you can sense the fullness and the emptiness, and no response arises within you to any of them, then there is completeness.

S: Is this the same as the witness?

AH: No. Witness comes before completeness. If you're complete, there may be awareness, but not necessarily. You can be complete without awareness, but awareness is inherent in witnessing. Awareness, let's say, is the step before completeness. It's as if there's a witnessing of everything without response, without being for or against. But witnessing will be experienced as a nothingness. Awareness is a kind of space. The experience of completeness is not necessarily an experience of space. You feel complete; your mind says you're complete. It's even more a sense that there is no movement that is predicated on incompleteness. There is not necessarily even the perception of completeness. You can be complete and not be conscious of it.

S: How do you do anything when you're in that state? When you're just being, what motivates you to act?

AH: Love. As well as the simple needs of the body, obviously. Also, the completeness does not act, see? It remains as you, your center. Your body and mind move and act, to do what's needed. As I said, being complete doesn't mean you sit down and vegetate.

S: I can't see how, if you are being, you can do.

AH: That's because you're thinking of your body as your self. You think that you're the body, and that if you just are, you won't do anything. In fact, your body will continue to move and do all kinds of things, that's its nature. But, if you know you're not your body, there doesn't need to be any change externally. You do what you do, or you do something else, it doesn't matter. You may take a bath, do the dishes, hang out or work hard, but who you are is in repose. It's as if there is a cyclone and you are at the center of it, always at the center of it. Things around the cyclone might move fast or slow, but it wouldn't affect you. Even when the cyclone is gone, the center remains.

S: Is it possible to reach the chasm of our incompleteness without working through all our holes?

AH: It's possible, but working through the holes is a very efficient way of coming to the chasm. Someone who has dealt with many holes and the ideas, beliefs, desires and fears that go with them, may at some point perceive that it doesn't seem necessary for them to work on the holes. But it would take a lot of work and depth of work to come to that perception. It possible to make such a jump, but it's not easy.

When you are complete, the action is love. Just as your body needs food and safety when you're taking care of it, your environment needs care when you're complete. From the perspective of completeness, the whole universe is your body. There's no separation, so you take care of it as an action of love. There is no sense of isolation, of feeling you are separate from other things and not caring about them. Love arises for everyone and everything.

We are conditioned to believe that we'll be motivated to do something only if we feel interested. Our mind is conditioned to believe that we won't take action unless we have some kind of investment, be it desire or fear or hope or preference one way or another. Right? If this is so, it means you're never being spontaneous. But the action of love is spontaneous. The moment you do something out of interest, it is not completely spontaneous; there's a little gap. You do something because of this or that. When you're complete, you don't do something because, you just do something; the action is a natural arising.

So there's no need for the discrimination of the mind: "This is good, this is bad." The knowledge is innate. You do what you do and it is the right thing. That's very different from how the mind functions, or the way the ego perceives things. The ego and the mind always think in terms of cause and effect, preferences and choices and time and results and categories. You do this because it is a good thing; you do that because it is needed. You do need your mind to do this type of thinking. But when you act from completeness, you act without the mind; you are completely spontaneous. The mind doesn't know how to do that.

Love will not flow spontaneously and continuously without that spontaneity. If your love is channeled through the categories of your mind, then love is not completely spontaneous and the heart is closed. If you are loving and helpful because you think it is the right thing to do, in some situations you might be actually helpful and in others not. But action which arises from completeness has nothing to do with such thinking. It is perception and action at the same time. It's completely on, always appropriate.

S: How is presence related to completeness?

AH: Presence is completeness. When you finally understand what presence is, when you're completely present, you are complete. There is the valuing of presence: there is the perception of completeness. When you're complete, you're content with being present. There's no need for anything else.

S: Can not valuing presence be a sign of incompleteness?

AH: Yes. When I say valuing presence, I mean being content with being a presence without thinking you're being present. It's a very simple thing, really. When you're content with anything, you're not thinking you're content, see? You think you're content only when you're going into the contentment or going out of it, since at those times there's a contrast. When you're completely content with being present, you're just present. However, if you are simply present, a person observing you from outside might say, "Oh, this person's content being present." Now, you're the one who's present. You're not thinking or feeling that you're present, you just are. It's very simple. You're just present. So, that's it. But, if you think of it in your mind, or someone else looks at it from outside, then there is an evaluation or conclusion about your state. The notion of being content is a concept that the mind creates to explain why the person is not doing something else. For the person who's complete and present, there is no need to conceptualize contentment. You conceptualize contentment only if you're not content. If human beings were always content, we'd have no idea or concept called contentment. If it's always present, you never conceptualize it. You don't need to separate it out from the rest of experience. Only when it's absent, can you become aware of it.

The same applies to completeness. If it is always there, you don't feel its absence, so you never conceptualize it.

S: Once in a while, I feel I'm really enjoying something. I'm enjoying it, but I'm not thinking about it. Then I become aware of it.

AH: That's the kind of thing I'm talking about. When you're really happy, you're happy and that's it. You're not even thinking or noticing that you are happy. Then at some point you do notice, and most of the time that's the beginning of something else, of self-evaluating mental activity. So, it's better when you're happy not to know and for no one else to notice either. You may be happily making dinner and someone says, "My, you look happy." And you wish they hadn't mentioned it. The mere awareness of your state can move you out of Being and into self-consciousness, but not necessarily.

S: There's no "I am"?

AH: There is "I am." Completeness is the experience of "I am" without mind, without anybody reflecting on it and saying "I am," without subjectivity. It is just the actual "I am-ness," without the mind conceptualizing it. "I am" is the same thing as presence, as the "I," as the true identity, except there is no need to conceptualize.

When you're complete you're not even interested in completeness. You're totally unself-conscious; you're not self-conscious at all. You're just self. And you cannot say really if it's self or not self, because these are concepts. The completeness is sometimes called self; sometimes it is called no self. Both can apply.

Completeness is a very simple, little thing. Very simple, very little, very minute, very uncomplicated. And at the same time it is without the huge gap between you and the universe. It is the state of no gap.

EIGHT

Supporting Self-Realization

Today we will discuss a matter of great importance for self-realization at any level. It is an obscure point that most of us are not aware of until we are suddenly confronted with it. With great chagrin we recognize that the state of self-realization cannot be sustained. I think many people fear this experience. Certain things seem to take the realization away, as if the rug gets pulled out from under us. And, in some sense, it is literally so—something gets pulled out from under you, and you fall. You can't keep the realization you had, or the sense of uniqueness. This can happen on any level of human actualization, from the most ordinary to the most refined kind of inner realization.

Half of the work of self-realization really has to do with the integration of support, not just attaining the state of realization. In order for realization to become a permanent attainment there needs to be support for realization. This is the reason it is possible to achieve a state of self-realization and to lose it—you don't have the support for it. This is the specific issue we are going to talk about today. We will discuss a practice that will help you integrate whatever realization arises, so that it does not get lost or taken away.

We typically grapple with this issue for a long time. We stay in the dark because the state that arises when the rug is pulled from under us is one of not knowing what to do about it. We expect that the state, condition, realization, or actualization of ourselves that we experience should just continue by itself. It seems to us that when we resolve or understand our issues about the state that is realized, we should be able to sustain it. It should become permanently attained; it should become what we call a station. But experience shows that this is not the case. It is possible to understand a certain state of realization completely and still not be able to embody it, to identify with it, or to be it in any permanent fashion.

States of self-realization can occur in many dimensions. Self-realization can be on the individual level, on any of the boundless dimensions, or on a non-dual level. The basic element common to experiences of realization in all the dimensions is a sense of not being concerned about reality, of not being concerned about who you are. There is a sense of certainty about yourself and about your perception of reality. It also manifests as a sense of completeness, as a sense of things making sense, as a sense of having meaning to yourself, to your life and to your world without necessarily knowing what that meaning is. Everything has an implicit sense of a meaning, value and preciousness; there is no questioning of it. Your life originates from this sense of meaningfulness, significance, and preciousness that is implicit and not questioned. Your life, your action, your activity and creativity originate from that pure and certain sense of significance to your world and who you are.

The sense of confidence, certainty, meaning, preciousness, and value implicit in the presence of a state of realization is not necessarily recognized. You just don't question; you just live life as if it is precious and has meaning. There isn't necessarily a particular meaning you can articulate. That's not the point. The sense of meaning is there because there is self-realization. You are there. Your very reality is present and you are it. The very reality of you, or whatever dimension of reality you are realized on at that time, is the significance, the meaning, the preciousness, and it gives everything about you and your world significance, meaning, and value.

When this sense of self-realization is absent you usually experience meaninglessness and emptiness in yourself and in your life. Nothing matters, nothing is important. You don't count. You don't know what you want to do, nothing that you want to do is important. You don't have any sense of what's right or what's not right; there is no innate sense of orientation, of direction, or of what is valuable to do.

The state of self-realization is better known by its absence than by its presence. When it is absent, you feel that you don't know who you are, you don't seem to exist. You feel that there is nothing to you: you don't matter, you aren't important. You feel insignificant, your life feels insignificant, you don't even know what you want to do. You wonder why you should even live. A person can become suicidal at this point. Why live? You feel that there is no point in living. In the absence of self-realization you feel a sense of hopelessness about yourself, your life and all of existence.

The ego personality deals with the loss of a sense of meaning by creating a sense of meaning. As we have seen, the usual personality or ego way of trying to create meaning is by having goals and aims that you will attain one of these days. The meaning of your life becomes the attainment of those goals. For most people life has meaning only in terms of these long term goals and hopes. Ego's way of dealing with the loss or absence of realization is to relegate it to the future. Sometime. And what the goals and the aims are doesn't matter; they could be anything. Your goal when you are young might be having the perfect relationship, and you might feel that if you have it everything will have meaning and significance and value and preciousness. Or you might have goals about your career, your work or some other attainment: scientific, artistic, or even enlightenment or realization. But all your thoughts are on the future, and your life has meaning and significance only from that perspective. That's the level of ego.

In the dimension of Essence there are experiences of self-realization in which meaning is based on the presence of the realized state in the present moment, rather than being based on the future. This eliminates the dependency on the future. Goals and aims become less and less important. In other words, the aim becomes the present moment, and the present moment is its own significance, is its own preciousness. The present moment is not different from the self-realization, which is not different from the self that is realized, which is not different from the reality that is precious.

Now the difficulty that I want to talk about here is not the issue of the self-realization itself, but that of permanently establishing the self-realization. The experience of self-realization is not unusual. Many people have it occasionally. However, making that state a station, making it a permanent attainment so that you don't lose it, is a different story. A bigger story. You can understand the issue somewhat by looking at self-realization from the perspective of the ego.

From the perspective of the ego, realization or actualization is the goal you have. And you live your life according to goals, aims and ideals. These ideals might even be unconscious. You may plan to be a doctor, so you devote twenty years of your life to becoming a doctor because you expect your career to give meaning to your life. Or you plan to be a movie star so you spend twenty years pursuing that. People are willing to go through a lot to reach their goals. They go through misery, through poverty, through humiliation, through all kinds of things. Their goal is the most important thing there is, and they believe that if they can't attain it there is no point to living.

What we want to see here is that for the ego those goals or aims give the person a sense of meaning or significance only if their environment and their relationships support them, and let them feel that their goals are important. If you have a goal and everyone around you thinks that it's not important, then that goal won't give you meaning. People usually choose goals and aims that are idealized by society. You use all of society to support your sense of meaning. Being a movie star, for instance, is supported by society as a whole. Everyone thinks it's a wonderful thing. They think it's great, it's creative. You can be creative, make money, be famous. There is a lot of support for it. If suddenly everyone around you is thinking that being a star is terrible, you will be very deflated. You will feel that all the twenty years or so you spent trying to get there have been a waste. You will probably have an identity crisis. Some people might even commit suicide.

This brings us to discussing friends as differentiated from enemies. In this case, a friend is a person who supports you in attaining your goals. An enemy is anyone who stands in your way or who takes your support away. In fact, generally speaking, that's how you choose friendships. You choose friends that support your point of view. If a friend doesn't support your view of life or reality or whatever is important, it is problematic. The relationship becomes difficult. You are disappointed and hurt and angry and frustrated. So a friend is someone who helps you and supports you in the attainment of your goals. An enemy will be seen as anyone who takes your support away from you, or puts barriers between you and your goal.

Now the same thing happens on the essential level. On the essential level, a state of self-realization will not continue if there is no support for it. Any state of realization is insecure and vulnerable as long as there is no support for it. From this perspective you can again see what a friend is and what an enemy is. A friend is anyone or anything that supports the state of self-realization; an enemy is anyone who takes it away or who creates barriers to the support of that self-realization. A friend or an enemy can be a person, an institution, a body of knowledge, or anything.

When support for self-realization comes from outside you, it comes from feeling that self-realization is precious, acknowledged and valued. Here, the greatest support comes from your teacher. This is why your teacher is your best friend. Your teacher is someone who not only helps you to attain that reality, but someone who can perceive it in you and knows it is a valuable thing. When you see that someone perceives your state, you feel seen, and you feel supported in that state. This is the reason everyone talks about wanting to be seen and not being seen, wanting to be appreciated and not being appreciated. All of it really has to do with support.

An enemy does not see you, or if he does see you, he tries to cut down what he sees instead of appreciating it. Someone who does not have self-realization will tend not to see it in you, and if they see something about it, they will tend to ignore it. You feel ignored and not seen, and lose your support. You feel there is nothing there to stand on. If you feel you are not seen, appreciated, or valued, then you will feel that your reality is not supported and it tends to become very vulnerable and can crumble at any moment.

So if you are on your own it is much more difficult to support yourself. Having someone there who can see you and says, "Oh, yes, I know her," makes you feel, "I am here, I can see it is wonderful, it's real." Otherwise you aren't sure whether it's real or not. You might be crazy; you don't know. If everybody says, "that's not how things are," you will be hard pressed not to doubt your reality. Absolute certainty in which you don't need any external perception or support does not happen until the final stage of inner realization. Until then there is a need, a very powerful need, for support of your realization, your reality. Ultimately a friend becomes a person who can see you, and not only see you, but appreciate what they see instead of trying to cut it down.

That is why we need the support of people who have a similar point of view when we are trying to realize reality, or a part of our reality that is not part of the common cultural point of view. In fact, you can look at yourself or at a person engaged in spiritual work in terms of their seriousness by looking at the kind of support they seek. Individuals who are really serious about their self-realization usually seek and find support for it. But individuals who do not seek and do not have that support for their self-realization usually want something else. I have spoken about this issue of support before in terms of physical needs, such as creating the right environment, the right financial security, the right structure and organization of life for yourself. This is part of the support that is needed, but support is also a much deeper thing.

For any state of self-realization there are issues about support which come from the past. As a child you may have felt that you were not seen, not appreciated, or not supported. For instance, you may not have been supported in recognizing your feelings. Or maybe no one cared about your feelings, or no one cared about your creativity. Any part of you that was not seen by your environment, or was seen and not appreciated, or was ignored or devalued, becomes unsupported. You feel that you cannot be that part, you cannot integrate it, you cannot manifest it, because there will be nothing to stand on.

Most of the time the totality of our Essence is not seen. When we are children, being our Essence is a very scary thing. We are very lonely, very alone as our Essence, and completely unsupported, so we create a sense of ourselves that our parents can support. That's how we get into image, performance, and external accomplishments that our parents can see and acknowledge, and hence support.

These issues from childhood arise when we begin to experience the state of self-realization. Every time an aspect of our Essence is realized, it brings up the lack of support that we experienced in childhood. These issues need to be explored and worked through. If they are not worked through, you will look for support in your present environment.

You might fall in love with someone who you feel sees you; you might associate with people who you feel see you and support you. These people might not be even seeing or supporting the real thing in you; they might be seeing and supporting something else, but you create the fantasy that they support you. When you realize finally that it isn't real, you feel hurt and deeply disappointed. You experience a deep sense of collapse and disintegration. When you feel that your support is taken away, which amounts to feeling that your real self doesn't exist, it brings a state of loss of self-realization which is a pointless, meaningless and deficient kind of emptiness. Wanting to be seen, wanting to be appreciated, wanting to be loved, these become very strong and powerful. You find out that you have become so sensitive that if anyone says something that indicates that they haven't seen you, you really feel it. You take it as a big insult when you say something and another person misinterprets it. It's not only an insult, but you are personally hurt, devastated. Your whole reality crumbles because you feel the lack of support.

Sometimes we go to great lengths trying to get support, trying to get someone to love us, to see us, to support us. As I said, for a long time you need to be in an environment that supports your realization. You need to have at least some contact with people who know the reality that needs to be supported, because you don't have your own support. If all the people around you are completely ignorant of that reality, you will find it difficult to realize that reality. And when you doubt it, the doubt by itself cuts away any support you have, and you lose your certainty. You are impressionable and not completely free, so you tend to believe people when they say, "That's not true," especially if they are people you care about. That's the way you get completely cut down. This is the state of not being seen and not being appreciated for who you are. And what it is to be seen and appreciated changes depending on the state you are realizing.

So we have talked about how not being seen is a problem for self-realization. What is the resolution? The resolution usually comes more from your enemies than from your friends. Your friends may support you, but they do not give you the ultimate support, support you can depend on. When you depend on a friend's support, you do not realize your own independent support.

So at some point it is useful and necessary to have only your own inner support which is not dependent on external sources. This means you have to have support for aloneness. You need to have support for the state of aloneness itself. And this is much more difficult to attain than the state of self-realization.

If your support for realization, for being your self and being real, is in your environment and you leave it to go off by yourself or with other people, you will feel you can't be the same way, because the support for being real depends on that environment. For instance, when you are with your teacher you might say, "I can be myself easily." Right? But if you go back to your business or talk to other people, it's gone. You can't be the same way. You begin to bring back your shell, your personality, in order to function in the world.

This is where your enemies become useful. An enemy is useful here because an enemy exposes the fact that you don't have your own inner support. By taking away your external support, your enemies show you the gap in yourself. They show you the hole in you. Now your enemy might be doing it because they want to teach you something, or they might be doing it because they hate you, or because they don't care about you, or because they are ignorant.

When someone cuts you down or undermines you or devalues you, your tendency is to feel hurt or rejected. But if you really feel the situation deeply, you will realize that you have lost your support, and you feel that you can't maintain your reality. The usual reaction is tremendous rage and hatred toward that person and you want to get revenge.

It is fine to see this. Such a reaction needs to be understood, experienced and integrated, but it won't give you support. Support will come only when you experience the state of no support, which is not an easy state to experience. It is not easy because it is the state of feeling you don't know what to do, don't know what's happening, haven't got the slightest idea of what's up or what's down. You feel there's no ground to stand on, no wall to lean against. You look around and there's nothing to hold on to. You wonder how you can help yourself and you feel you can't. That's the state of no support. The state of no support is the state of "I can't help myself." You want to put your feet on something but there is a huge emptiness underneath you. There's nothing to put your feet on. You need some ground to support your reality, but nothing is there. So you try to hold on and the tension brings back the personality with its defenses, and the result is anger, rage, and hatred. This state is not easy. It leaves you feeling deficient, helpless, unable, not knowing, worthless, and weird. It is a state of loss of all support, all capacity. It is only by learning to stay in that state and tolerating it that true support will arise.

Like other essential aspects, associated with this aspect of support is a hole that is experienced as lack of support. Most of the time an enemy is the right person to expose it for you. Sometimes your friends love you too much to expose it in you. Your friends may be aware that you need to depend on them less, but they may not have the heart to do anything about it. But you might find an enemy who will do something about it. This is why a teacher is sometimes seen as an enemy. A teacher sometimes precipitates this state just by confronting you with its reality. If your teacher confronts your fake support and your dependency that needs support, usually you'll hate your teacher for a while. Or you'll hate your friends if your friends support you in that way. You'll see your friends or teacher as an enemy and in some sense they are an enemy. That's the definition of an enemy, but it is a useful enemy. So your teacher sometimes seems to be your friend and sometimes seems to be your enemy. I am not saying you should go around looking for enemies. There are a lot of enemies around without looking for them. Things will just happen. A lot happens in our world and in our environment that exposes lack of support.

Sometimes it takes a long time to encounter your lack of support, but it always happens at some point. When you really let yourself experience the hole, the deficiency, the emptiness, without trying to get support or to be seen or to be mirrored, you will see yourself, and this is the way you will get support. Support usually occurs through mirroring. Anyone can support you by mirroring you. Mirroring involves someone showing you what you are by seeing and appreciating you.

True support is not mirroring, and arises only when you confront your lack of support, the absence of it, which is there already like a huge abyss. A huge, humungous abyss, a humungous hole into which you go and become a nothingness. If you allow yourself to feel it, then true support will arise in you. When true support comes you feel as if you are sitting on a mountain top. The whole mountain becomes like a fountain of support for your reality. From within, you feel an immensity, a tremendous immensity, a tremendous presence, a tremendous existence that is almost as hard as rock, and it supports whatever reality you have realized.

At the beginning, your teacher embodies that support, embodies that immensity, that mountain, and you feel supported. This is why you are able to have experiences of self-realization when you are with your teacher or with any realized teacher. The teacher is the supporting mirror, the true supporting mirror. The support is there in the environment, so it is possible for you to experience Essence in various states. It is as if the support already exists.

However, when you leave, you find it difficult to sustain because you have no support for it. Support is there, but it is not yours yet. To make it yours, you must internalize it, not just use your teacher for support. This happens by working through the issues that block support in you. These issues are usually nothing but experiences of loss of support in the past, and ways of projecting it and trying to get it externally.

Most of the work on support happens on issues involving other people or careers or interests. Many of your problems with people and relationships have to do with this issue of support. Many of your hurts, many of your rejections, and much of your anger and hatred have to do with these issues. You interact with someone, something happens and you feel you are not supported. Someone says something and you feel they are taking away your support. They might or might not have intended to take your support away. Either way, one of the deepest attacks is when someone says or does something that takes away your support. You might experience something real and tell it to your friend and your friend misinterprets it. They think it means something else.

You might feel hurt and experience what has happened as a loss of support. You feel undermined. This happens a lot. It can happen on all levels and in very subtle ways. It is tricky. Little things can have devastating consequences. You can have an interaction with someone or an interaction with the environment that seems to be unimportant, and for a whole week afterward you realize you are feeling lost and you don't know why. When you trace it back, you remember that a certain person looked at you in a way that indicated she didn't appreciate you when you were being yourself and that brought about the emptiness, the hole of support. Little by little your external supports will drop away. And as external supports drop away you will feel more and more alone. Feeling alone means that you are integrating your own support. You do not need external support. You do not need props. One of the supports that might fall away in the beginning might be your career. Your career might support your sense of identity and your sense of value, so at some point you have to become free from it. Or your support might come from love relationships or friendships, and at some point you need to become free from that support. You may realize that you get support from the group you are in so you need to become aware of that and become free from it. This will bring even more aloneness and more independence. At some point you realize that you are using the teaching you are following for support and you will have to drop that as a support. This will bring an even bigger aloneness. And the aloneness will continue.

The more it is integrated and the more inner support is realized, the more your experience of self-realization will become independent and permanent. At some point you will have to become independent of the school and of the teacher. This does not mean to be physically separated. You can be in the school and still be independent and alone. Eventually you will have to be free from all teaching, from everything you have learned, everything, absolutely everything. You will have to give up all the ways you support your self-realization with anything you have learned in the past, so that nothing from the past is needed for support. The past can only support self-image. Your self-realization will deepen, go to different levels and become more permanent.

The final support that has to go is your mind. Even after you let go of your particular teaching, or whatever you learned from other sources, you still have your own insights and your own experiences. They define your way of looking at things and of understanding things. "This is me, this is that, that's the meaning of this." These are the final supports that have to go.

Then you can be who you are, self-realized without even having to know it. Self-realization does not become complete and permanent until it doesn't need any external support at all, not even the support of your thoughts. You don't even need to recognize it. You don't need to feel it, just experience the natural thing. You are the presence without cognizing the presence. Letting go of the teaching and letting go of your mind are the deepest, subtlest levels.

These are difficult issues that we are talking about, but they can be seen, understood, and worked through. And the process of working through them is actually the realization of the support that will ultimately make you independent. Any questions?

Student: When do people usually start encountering this issue?

A.H. Almaas: These issues of support happen at all levels. Whatever dimension or level you experience—fake or not fake, real or more real—this issue is there and you have to deal with it. It's not something to complain about, because there is no way to avoid it. I am not just creating an issue out of nowhere. It's an issue that is already there—one you experience all the time.

When you lose a lot of money, or a loved one or a relative, you feel a loss of support. Sometimes, you don't just feel hurt and sad, you disintegrate. You think you've lost your identity. You lose your sense of self, your sense of meaning. What does losing money have to do with the meaning of your life? If you lose your child or your mother or your husband what does that have to do with the meaning of your life? But people do lose the meaning of their life. Their life crumbles because they have lost their support.

S: It seems like some of the things that we usually think of as bad, like getting fired or divorced, could actually be positive.

AH: Exactly. These are times when you can gain your own support. That's why people sometimes become stronger after a big loss. They get stronger because they have struggled with the issue correctly and found their own support. Other people get weaker after a big loss and they increasingly disintegrate. Those are the people who didn't manage it as well.

S: What do you mean by "struggling with the loss correctly"?

AH: The usual way that people handle a loss of support is by trying to find it in other relationships, trying to find it in another career, another situation, another belief, or another philosophy. That's the usual way. The real way to find your own support is to live in a way that will support what you know. Right? So feeling the lack of support will help you feel the true support and believe in it. If you do that then it is possible for you to regain your own support. When you can see and understand the truth of the situations in your life, the truth will be your support. Finding your true support means true nature has become your refuge.

S: Are you saying that most of the things that people do to take care of themselves when something bad happens to them are really cop-outs?

AH: It's a cop-out a lot of the time. People just don't know any better. It's not taught in schools. Schools don't teach us about support. Parents don't teach about support. Everybody talks about support, but there are no schools for it so people do the best they can. It takes a tremendous amount of integrity and sincerity for a person to see through these things about themselves on their own without opting for external supports. Eventually what it means to not opt for external supports is to not care about consequences; it may even mean that you don't care whether you live or die.

S: Can someone who is your friend become your enemy by not supporting you?

AH: Your friends become enemies when you feel they are not supporting you. In a sense, this also happens every time you understand something that your friend doesn't understand. Your friend can become your enemy in that moment. Your friend may just not understand. He or she may not do it deliberately. But you can't help feeling hatred and rejection toward your friend anyway.

S: You said that when someone does something that takes away your support you feel anger and hatred toward them; I was wondering whether the hatred and the anger are really directed at your own fear rather than at the person who isn't supporting you?

AH: You might direct it at the fear, but usually the hurt, the hate and the anger are directed at whoever hurt you. The objective of hate is to inflict a similar wound on the source of your pain. It's called revenge, and it has to be exactly the same kind of wound in order to be satisfying. Same kind, same intensity, and same place.

S: I'd like to understand the dynamics of what happens when you want to get revenge. It seems to feed on itself and that's what blocks feeling the lack of support.

AH: Right. And it blocks the hurt, too. The anger and the hatred block the hurt, the feeling of the wound. And you have to feel the hurt and the wound to feel the absence of support. The hatred and the anger are a reaction which help you avoid dealing with the issues. There is almost always hurt or a feeling of powerlessness under the hatred. Anger gives you a kind of strength and hatred gives you a kind of power. You react with anger and hatred, so you don't feel the sense of weakness and deflation. You can feel strong and powerful even though you are hurt.

There are many movies where the hero's only purpose in life is to get revenge; they are very popular movies. The old western movies are an example. The Indians come and kill the family, and then the dad goes out to find the ones who did it, and that gives meaning to his life. The story about the Count of Monte Cristo is the same. Hatred is the only thing left to fill the life of the person so the only thing that gives them meaning is revenge. Revenge gives you a big orgasm.

S: Isn't part of what you are calling revenge just a desire to enlighten the person who hurt you? To show them that they didn't see you or didn't appreciate you so they will be enlightened?

AH: For some people revenge is also an attempt to make the other person see them. That is what you are calling enlightenment. You feel hurt because the person didn't see you, so you want to make them see what they didn't see before. You want to rub their face in the mud until they see, until they realize that you are better than they thought you were. And it might be true that you are better than they thought you were, but you are still trying to make them see it in a revengeful way. You are both getting your revenge and still wanting the support.

Often the revenge for not being seen is that you want to hurt the other person or change them, so that they finally acknowledge that you're right. Sometimes nothing short of that will be satisfying. You will do everything in your power to destroy the other person, so they will finally admit the truth. Admit the truth that they didn't see who you were. But it's still revenge. All these feelings are very deep in human beings. A person can be dying and still be involved in it.

S: Is there a connection with holding grudges? Holding grudges seems like it could be a less active way of getting revenge.

AH: That's right. It is a quieter, milder form of revenge. For instance, you might just not talk to someone, you might ignore them or pretend they don't exist because that's what they did to you. You don't call them, or when you see them on the street, you don't say hello, and the person seems hurt the way you were hurt.

S: What's a good way to resolve the situation? If you associate with a person who never sees you and you feel hurt, how can you resolve it without holding a grudge?

AH: You can communicate with the other person. You can defend yourself, because that kind of interaction can be a form of attack. If it turns out that they feel attacked, you can be gentle and compassionate and try to explain it to them. But if it doesn't work, what else can you do? When things don't work, people usually separate.

These situations can be very normal, mundane situations. For instance, a woman might believe she's not pretty unless someone tells her she's pretty. And someone might tell her there is something wrong with her nose, and right away she starts thinking about plastic surgery. Everyone else has told her that she is beautiful, but one person says one thing about her nose and that's it. That shows that she has no support for that belief in herself. All her support is external, so a little hurt exposes a huge emptiness underneath.

S: Is it true that most people never see you? How can you defend against that without defending constantly?

AH: Not being seen is different from being actively attacked. It's true that you can walk down the street and people don't see you, but usually it is not important for those people to see you. It's more important for people with whom you have some kind of relationship to see you. They are the ones who upset you. Anyone can do something that hurts you, but not as easily as someone who is really close to you. That's why you need to work on your relationships.

S: What does having your own support mean in terms of Essence?

AH: It's a dimension of Essence called the diamond will. It's a deeper thing that has to do with the Hara and the lower belly more than anything else. The Hara is the support and at some point a certain realization, a certain aspect develops there. You feel a sense of solidity, sense of immensity, a sense of power and firmness that somehow supports you, supports your sense of self. Usually lack of support is experienced in the belly and the lower extremities. Some people feel that they don't have legs or that their legs are weak or wobbly. Or the belly feels like jello.

S: If you need to really experience lack of support to get support, what do you do for support while you are working on getting it?

AH: Your support increases with experience and understanding. Understanding the situation can be supportive. But, ultimately, the way you experience essential support is by giving in, by surrendering to the situation. You can't just trade lack of support for support. If you are experiencing a state of no support, you cannot have an inner experience of support. It is like letting yourself be under the influence of the inner resources. That's why I say it is a very difficult thing to deal with.

S: Why is it so difficult to work on?

AH: It's difficult because the hole has been there for so long. It is difficult to tolerate the painful feelings related to it. It's also very difficult to understand accurately. Most people misinterpret the various affects associated with this issue, because the meaning is new and subtle.

When you experience no support in the presence of someone like your teacher, it is easier to go through it. In time you can go through it by yourself because you already know you have gone through it many times. But even the idea that you can do it is a very slender thread, and it can break.

For true self-realization you have to jump. You have to take the risk of jumping when there is no support, when you have no idea of what's going to happen. It feels like jumping into an abyss. You don't know whether you are going to come out of it or not, or whether you'll be better or worse, or whether you'll come out of it the same kind of person or not. You don't know whether it will work or not. You have no idea. That is why a deep faith in reality, a basic trust in truth, can be very helpful at this point.

When the hole is experienced completely, true support will arise. Basically, true support is resisted by the attempt to hold on, which is why the true support of Essence cannot be faked. It is very difficult to really let go; you cannot be lazy about it. You can experience all kinds of states without doing much work, but not true support. Even certain self-realizations can happen without much work, but to experience true support your work has to be real.

When the support is integrated, you become independent. You do not need the external supports. The lack of mirroring from outside, not being seen correctly and appreciated by others, no longer affects you. The most that can happen when you are not seen is that your inner essential support will arise at such times. Your self-realization becomes a permanent attainment, a station. You are truly your beingness, regardless of the absence or presence of external feedback. You have support now in your alone space, in the aloneness of your mind.

NINE

The Dilemma of Boundaries

Today we'll talk about a certain dilemma which, by its very nature, is self-perpetuating. This dilemma comes from a certain belief about yourself, a certain way that you take yourself to be, which creates a lot of your suffering. The belief is that you are a separate and isolated individual with your own mind, your own likes and dislikes, your own body, your own will, your own history, your own tastes, beliefs, ideas, and knowledge. People consistently have a sense of being separate.

If you look at this belief, you'll see that it is basic to your perception of yourself and the world at large. This belief is so fundamental that you don't question it. How else could you be? Of course I am an individual separate from everyone else; otherwise, how could I drive my car? The mere fact that

I drive my car to a certain place indicates that I am separate from everyone else who drives other cars to other places. The perception is accurate; the conclusion is not. The perception is that we see a physical body moving into a car and driving it to a certain place. That is true. But why assume that you are that body?

Let's explore how this is a dilemma. First of all, if you take yourself to be an individual separated from the rest of the universe by your skin, which is the boundary that most people use to define themselves, then a certain issue arises between you and others, as well as between you and society, you and the world, you and the universe, you and God. And this issue is: "What am I going to get from the other?" Right? If you assume you are bounded by the boundaries of your body, you are bound to feel scared of others and to want something from them.

That is the dilemma, and it is self-perpetuating because you are constantly trying to make what is inside the boundaries stronger, better, more powerful. You are constantly trying to fill it with things from outside. But when your actions are motivated by fear or wanting, they strengthen the boundaries, because you are acting from the assumption that boundaries exist. The stronger your sense of boundaries becomes, the more you feel isolated and scared and the more you feel that you want things, or that others want things from you. You feel a sense of conflict between yourself and others: "What do the others have that I haven't got? What have I got that they haven't got? Is what they have better than what I have? Or maybe what I have is better." This is the beginning of issues about comparison, jealousy, and competition.

What I'm saying now is only from the perspective of social relations. If you think of your life in relation to other people, you will see that the basis of all the things you complain about is the belief that you are a separate individual. How can you be scared of someone unless you believe you are distinct and isolated from them? How can you want anything from anyone without believing you are separate from them? This is how the belief in separateness brings about all the social emotions.

Because that sense of separation in itself is suffering, a deep longing to dissolve the separation, a deep longing to unite or merge with something or someone, develops. The boundaries themselves become a frustration, become pure suffering. The strong desire to bridge that gap, to melt the boundaries manifests most often in wanting to be close to or to connect to someone else so that you won't feel the separation. You try to dissolve the isolation by engaging in the activity of desire. You want love; you want acceptance. You want someone to love you, or you want to love someone. But wanting to love or to be loved, that in itself implies the belief that you are a separate individual.

So believing you are a separate individual, you try not to be separate. But how can you merge, how can you dissolve your boundaries when your actions are based on a belief in separation? Can a longing for union bring about union? Can attempts to merge bring about merging? Your actions create the dilemma. You want to be united with someone or something because you believe you are separate, and you act accordingly. But acting accordingly strengthens your separateness, so you continue to be a separate individual, an island.

And by being separate, you cannot be generous. You believe that you can only be generous if your island is well-stocked and well-protected. Your basic posture is of self-protection, self-replenishment, holding on. That is the root of selfishness. How can you help being selfish if you believe yourself to be separate?

When I say these things I'm not implying that you should simply believe that you are not separate and everything will be fine. So far I'm only describing what is happening. Don't jump to the conclusion that you should begin tearing apart your boundaries. Just wanting to tear apart your boundaries indicates that you believe you are a separate individual. You need to have boundaries in order to reject them. There has to be someone separate there for anything to be rejected. Right? If you say "no" to anything, even to your boundaries, you're creating boundaries.

If you are an individual with boundaries that distinguish you from others and from everything else, in addition to the attitudes of fear, desire, comparison, competition, and greed, you will also have a fear of death. Fear of harm is one thing; fear of death is another. If you take yourself to be a body that is separate from other bodies, you are bound to feel scared of death. You know you will die some day. One of these days you will go to sleep and never wake up. You will never return to the vertical position.

Just realize how much fear there is in being a separate individual. Realize how much longing there is for that fear to disappear. Realize how much you do in your life to try to deal with that fear and that longing. What if it isn't true that you are a separate individual? If it isn't true, then everything you do is pointless. And it is not only pointless, but it perpetuates the dilemma.

A basic mistake that the mind makes is basing all its beliefs on physical facts. If something seems to have physical boundaries, then it must be a fact that it exists only within those physical boundaries. We see the form and we think our inner experience must correspond with it. Our body is this size; our inner experience must be the same. This is a basic, implicit assumption.

Why? Why does consciousness have anything to do with size or appearances, with boundaries? Why is your consciousness bounded by what your eyes see? Look at a cat, for instance. Do you believe that a cat experiences itself to be the size that you see? You do! What if that isn't true? What if a cat doesn't experience itself as having any size? You assume that a cat experiences itself as that size, because that's how you see the size of the cat.

Similarly, you see yourself as a certain size, so you say, "I am this big." It's a basic assumption that you never question. You assume that the form that you see should define how your consciousness experiences itself. In other words, you're making your consciousness, your inner sense of who you are, correspond to the form that your eye sees; you're making it correspond to physical reality. But who says having a small body and an infinite consciousness is contradictory? There is no logic that says it can't be so.

We are seeing some basic assumptions and their consequences. I want you to question, to investigate these assumptions. Don't just immediately say, "These beliefs are wrong." First realize that you do have these beliefs, and although you never consciously thought them before now, you do firmly believe in them. They are so implicit that you usually don't think about them. You just act. See that you actually feel: "Yes, I have boundaries here and here and here that are exactly the same size as my body. Of course, they should be there, because my body is." You need to work on being aware of your boundaries, because they are usually unconscious. They are the basic axioms of your identity. Be aware of the axiom that you are inside those boundaries, that you are what is inside your skin. Pay attention and you'll see what is actually you.

You don't need to say that your beliefs about boundaries are wrong; you don't need to do anything about them except be aware of them. See what happens when you are aware that you are experiencing yourself as boundaries. You may find out that you do not consider it an assumption that you have boundaries; you consider it a fact. That's alright, just be aware that you consider it a fact. Maybe it's true that it is a fact. Just realize that that is what you think, and that all your thinking and all your living are based on it.

Just be aware of your experience while you are looking at me and listening to me. Don't you assume that there is a you, who stops right there and listens to me, who stops right here? What if I don't think of myself as stopping right here? What are you seeing then? Only your assumption. And you don't know that it is an assumption; you take it to be an absolute fact. You take it to be reality.

Some of you may be getting a little jittery. You may be thinking, "Wait a minute, if I don't have boundaries, what will happen to what is inside of me? It will just float all over. There will be nothing left of me." But that assumes that you are someone bounded by boundaries. The fear that you are going to disappear is caused by the boundaries. You cannot be afraid of disappearing, if you don't believe you are separate. When you say "I will disappear," what do you mean by "I"? You have to believe that you are separate to be afraid of losing your boundaries.

Sometimes you experience being full; other times it's being little and deflated. The membrane of your boundaries makes you into a balloon. Why isn't it possible to look at your body and say that it is here, and then feel yourself and say *you* don't end anywhere? What's wrong with that? Why do you have to make your feeling of yourself stop where your body ends? Why? Why make that assumption? Why not question it? See if it holds up under scrutiny.

So we are pointing to certain things that we think are facts, and I'm saying that they are assumptions. You don't need to believe they are assumptions. Just single out the facts and look at them. Scrutinize them. Try to understand them. And remember that boundaries are not dissolved by trying to do anything about them. The moment you try to do anything, you are believing you are a separate individual who has his or her own volition, and that strengthens the boundaries.

If you are aware of the boundaries, just aware of them—you will also be aware of the individuality that is created by the boundaries. You will be aware of the problems, conflicts, and suffering of that individuality that thinks of itself as a person with boundaries. If you see that it is what you have taken yourself to be throughout your life, it is possible that within that simple awareness, there can arise compassion for the suffering that is caused by those beliefs. Just look at the suffering of that person, the pain of that person. When you see the assumptions of that individuality and all the things those assumptions have caused it to go through, there can arise a compassion; there can arise a love.

You may see that this individuality has no bad intentions. It is just ignorant; it doesn't know. It is taking itself to be something and by merely believing that, all its experience emerges from it. It is jailing itself, creating its own prison, and it doesn't know what to do about it. And just by wanting to do something about it, it strengthens the walls of its own cage.

It is only the compassion and love that spontaneously arise from the perception of the facts that have a capacity to dissolve the boundaries. That's why when we want to cross our boundaries, we try to do it through love. We want a lover. But we go about it in the wrong way—we try to love someone, try to get someone to love us.

We don't let ourselves see that these are assumptions that we take to be facts or that suffering results from them. We have taken ourselves to be separate individuals all of these years, and we have been doing everything that we can to free ourselves from that trap. But we aren't free, because we don't know what to do. We're hopelessly trapped, because our knowledge is based on assumptions. When you see that the individuality that you have taken to be you all these years is trapped and really cannot free itself, from that arises compassion and love.

And when the love arises, you will see that the love is you, is your very nature. When you see that the love is you, you will see that there are no boundaries, and that love is also everyone else. Love is the consciousness of everyone, and that consciousness, which is love, has nothing to do with boundaries. The moment it is there, there are no boundaries. The other person is love so what does loving them or not loving them mean?

When you finally see that you are love, that everyone is love, there's no need for hoarding, there's no need for competition, there's no need to fear anyone else. There's no need to reject or react to rejection. What will you reject? You could reject another person's body, if you take that person to be his body, but when you know that the person is love, what would you reject? Rejecting someone else is rejecting yourself; it's the same thing. Loving someone is loving yourself, loving love, which is nothing but being love.

Become aware of your individuality, aware of your sense of being an individual that is bounded by skin and a body, and aware of how that individual has a whole world, a whole history, a whole universe that is full of action, interaction, suffering, fear, and desire. If you can be aware of all that, what is aware of all that is your consciousness, which is love.

You're usually trapped, you see, in being one part of that individual, one feeling, or one role reacting to another role. You don't let yourself be or see the whole thing. You take yourself to be an individual who has certain boundaries, limitations, will, volition, mind, and opinions, decisions, history, preferences, relationships and all that. When you see that individual, then look at who is looking, realize who is seeing. It's your true consciousness. That's you as love, you as conscious love.

Student: How does being conscious love affect how you relate to people who are close to you? Do you love everyone the same?

A.H. Almaas: When you realize that you are love and everyone is love, that doesn't mean that you won't feel a special love for your wife or your child. It doesn't mean that you consider your wife exactly the same as everyone else. On that level of consciousness everything is love. But there are also other kinds of love that are more personal, that don't have to do with boundaries, just as love is not the only manifestation of Being that can be experienced as boundless. It is, however, the specific aspect that dissolves boundaries in an easy and effortless way.

S: Does the boundlessness take away your sense of individuality?

AH: When you realize your true nature, there is a true individuality that is based on the fact of boundlessness. It looks as if it has boundaries, but it doesn't have the feeling of boundaries. This individuality is based on love, instead of the usual individuality which is based on rejection.

S: When I try to sense my boundaries, they don't dissolve. I'm not sure I'm really doing it. Is there anything I can do to work on this?

AH: Yes, you need to sense your arms and legs for a long time in order to bring an awareness of your boundaries into your consciousness. That needs to happen first. When I sense my arms and legs, I feel my arms and legs, but I also sense myself, which is both inside and outside my body. There is both an awareness in the arms and legs and an awareness of my own consciousness.

S: I have a hard time seeing what you mean by boundlessness. Is it possible for you to describe it?

AH: You don't see boundlessness by trying to see it, by trying to eliminate your boundaries. You don't see a boundary and then realize that it doesn't exist. You only see the boundlessness when you see the boundaries and let yourself be—then you see there is no boundary. It's not an act of rejecting boundaries, nor an act of dismantling them. It's not even an act of perception.

You see boundlessness by being boundlessness. You just are. That beingness itself is the experience of no boundaries.

Being doesn't have boundaries. When you feel the boundary, you are the boundary. When you are the love, you are your loving consciousness. Then there are no boundaries.

It feels somewhat like humility. It's a humility, a gentleness, a softness, a lightness, an acceptance, a compassion. Love is the breath of the boundless Being. It pervades all existence and melts all boundaries in sweetness and gentleness. Love is the caring arms of Being holding all beings, letting them rest, let go, and merge with the boundless.

TEN

Knowledge and the Good

One way that we can describe what we are doing here is to say that we are engaged in the attempt to solve the mystery of life. Each person at some point needs to solve that mystery for himself. The mystery about our lives can manifest in various ways. One way it manifests is that we are concerned with questions like, What is it all about? Why am I here? Who am I? How do I get what I want? What is the purpose of life? What is worth doing?

Every once in a while we have a discussion that might advance our inquiry a few inches. Don't be too optimistic about it, though; it's not a simple thing, as you know. Very few people feel that they've solved the mystery of life. Today we will talk about one element that is necessary if we are going to solve the mystery of life for ourselves.

What we will talk about is the question of knowledge. We've been much concerned with knowledge here, but never explicitly talked about it. We will talk about knowledge itself, and try to come to a more correct perspective about knowledge—what knowledge is, what its use is, and how necessary it is for our lives. The word "knowledge," like so many other words, has been so bastardized that by now different people understand it to mean different things, most of which have nothing to do with the original meaning.

So our questions about knowledge begin with "What is knowledge?" When we say the word "knowledge," what do we mean? And our second question, "How important is it for us?" will depend on our answer about what it is. When we know what it is we will know its value. Knowledge is important in an obvious way because the mind is the overriding factor in our lives. Our mind determines what kinds of things we choose to do, what we discard, what we feel, what we think, what kind of a life we have.

By mind, I don't necessarily mean just our thoughts; I mean the totality of the psyche. The mind acts according to what it knows, or thinks it knows. A simple example is that when you want something, you try to get it because you think it is good for you. If you don't believe it is good for you, you won't try to get it. It's as simple as that. When I called this talk "Knowledge and the Good," I meant that usually everybody does what they think is good. At every moment of our lives, what we are engaged in depends on our belief about what is good for us or others.

Even the killer, or the thief, is doing what he thinks at the moment is a good thing to do. The thief who goes and robs a bank clearly thinks it's a good thing for him to do. At that moment it seems the best thing to do. Otherwise he wouldn't do it.

That's the first thing I want to establish: everyone does what he believes at that moment to be the good. In his book

Protagoras, Plato elaborates on this point, that everyone does the good. This point may not seem obvious; you may think of experiences in which you are acting or reacting in a certain way, and thinking, "Why am I doing that? It seems to be harmful." But you are rather compulsive about doing it. This might indicate that maybe we don't always do what we believe is good for us. But with deeper investigation you will see that, in fact, what you are doing depends on a belief about what is good that is unconscious at that moment.

So we see that the conviction that what we're doing is what is good can be either conscious or unconscious. Even someone who is being self-destructive thinks at some level that is what's good. Someone who commits suicide does so because it seems like the best thing to do. You may not be convinced of this principle; think about it more and perhaps you will see that, even though it might not appear so on the surface, any human being will do only what he thinks to be good.

The moment we realize that we always do what we believe to be good, we can begin to appreciate the value of knowledge. We think that something is good based on what we believe we know. If someone is furiously engaged in the pursuit of wealth, and willing to sacrifice everything for it, that person obviously believes that's a good thing for him or her to do. It is important to realize that this depends on previous knowledge: that person obviously believes that money will make him happy. But what if this belief isn't true? Maybe that person is unhappy because of something totally unrelated to money. So what, then, is the value of that person's frantic efforts to make money? If the point is to make him happy, it's a waste of time.

We can see that this person needs knowledge. He needs to know what is making him miserable. There is a belief that the misery is because he or she is poor. But what if this knowledge is not accurate? If it is not true, then that person is wasting his time trying to get the million dollars.

The million dollars will get this person something, but it will not necessarily give him what he thought he was going to get.

He believed that he knew something—he believed that money would make him happy. But if he had investigated that knowledge at the beginning, he might have found out that the cause of his misery was not poverty, and maybe would have saved the twenty years of furious activity. Maybe he would have done something else with his life.

Student: Are you saying that good and happy are the same thing?

A.H. Almaas: Most people equate them. Let's say that the good includes the happy. It's a larger category.

I think it is now clear that knowledge is the basis for what we do in our lives. Even to do the simple things in life, like brushing our teeth, requires knowledge. If we didn't know that brushing our teeth is beneficial, we wouldn't do it. But if we realize that without doing it, we get cavities and suffer, then we start doing it. What made us start brushing our teeth? Knowledge! We found out that it is good for us to brush our teeth, so we do it.

Of course, some people hear about the consequences of not brushing their teeth but still don't do it, so you might argue that they really don't want to do what is good for them. That is not necessarily true. A person might know that it's good for him to brush his teeth, but he might think it's a waste of time because he's so busy earning his first million dollars. He's thinking of what he thinks is a greater good. Or maybe he wants to sleep later in the morning instead of getting up in time to brush his teeth. He believes then that sleep is better for him at that moment.

I'm emphasizing how important knowledge is, because we don't usually see its value in our lives. We want to really see in the specific details of our lives, how we act according to what we know, or what we think we know.

Let's suppose you're married, and you like your husband. If you became completely convinced that another man is really better for you than your husband, you would probably leave your husband for that man. But if you stick with your husband, it is because you believe that doing that is the best thing for you at this time. Even people who are unhappy in their marriages stay there because they believe that this is the best they can do. Even if you stay in your marriage because you love your husband or wife, you are obviously still operating on certain assumptions: you believe that loving him or her is a good thing, that loving someone is good, and that staying with someone you love is the best thing to do.

Suppose your girlfriend doesn't want to see you for a week and you feel angry. Obviously you believe that being angry at her is the best thing for you. You believe you should be angry and hassle her until she changes her mind. You wouldn't act this way unless you thought that it would lead to the best thing for you. If you didn't think it was the right thing, you wouldn't get angry. This is true of all your emotional reactions in any situation.

So we're seeing the power of our minds to determine our lives, in every detail, from brushing our teeth, to interacting with mates, to doing our careers. Our minds determine how we want to be, what we want to do, everything, really, about how we live our lives.

So we have established two points: First, we do what we believe to be the good; and second, everything we do, every little thing, depends on what we think we know. When we realize these two points, it becomes easy to know what we are doing here: we are trying to find the correct knowledge of what is good and what is not good. What is really good for you? Is your belief about what is good for you true? Is what you believe to be the best way to do things really the best way?

S: Can an action always be traced back to what you believe is good for you, or can it ever be traced back to what you believe is good for someone else?

AH: It depends on the person. Most people do what is good for them, even if they think sometimes it's for the good of the other, as in self-sacrificing or self-effacing behavior. A more selfless person might choose what is good for the other, but still it is the good that is guiding the action. This is the thrust of what I am saying. Ultimately what is good is good for everyone, and the distinction between what's good for you or for another disappears, and only what is good remains. That is why I'm calling this talk "Knowledge and the Good."

Perhaps one morning you wake up and feel a little movement in your belly. If you've never felt anything like that before, you might react with fear, believing that something is wrong, and decide to go to the doctor; or you might ignore it and go back to sleep. Both reactions are based on supposed knowledge: if you are afraid and worried, you believe something is wrong; if you ignore it, you believe it is unimportant. However, if you knew that there was an energetic center there called the Kath or Hara, and that sometimes energy bubbles there, then you would recognize that feeling and say, "Ah, nice, my Hara is open today."

So your reaction depends on your knowledge. Suppose a person feels a stabbing pain or hurt in the chest, in the heart. He's never felt anything like this sensation before. He becomes alarmed: "Oh, I might be having a heart attack." Or maybe he'll be less alarmed but still want to get rid of the pain, so he says, "Oh, I'm hurting, I'm in pain, give me some Valium." But a person with a different perspective, a different knowledge, might react differently when he feels the hurt: "I must be feeling hurt, oh good, let me feel it, let me explore it." And if he feels the hurt for a while, he will begin to feel soft and gentle and warm inside himself.

This person had the knowledge that it isn't helpful to turn away from his pain, that when he is willing to feel the pain some kindness toward himself will arise.

It seems clear that we should do our utmost to gain the necessary knowledge for living our lives—to have what we want, to do what is actually good, to live a happy life, to really find out the meaning of life, to actually solve the riddle. To accomplish these things we clearly need the correct knowledge. Otherwise we do things believing them to be what they are not, such as marrying someone believing we love them, when we really married them because they reminded us of our mother.

We can see how much wasted effort there is in our lives, and how much suffering results. If we believe we're pursuing the good and it turns out not to really be good, it is because we took our knowledge for granted. We believe our own beliefs too much, without questioning them, and then go about our lives based on them.

I think I've given enough examples now for us to see that we might be wrong much of the time. And if we are wrong, and really don't know the truth of a situation, we are bound to suffer and waste our time. The best thing we can do for ourselves is to find the truth—not a general truth, but one that is specific to that situation and that moment. Is this thing I want really the good? Where did I learn that this is a good thing? Did the person I learned it from know it was the good? It was good for that person, but is it good for me?

Usually we don't ask these questions. We take whatever knowledge we have absorbed throughout our lives to be ultimate knowledge, and we act on it. Most of the knowledge we've acquired has become part of our minds as commandments, as absolute truth.

Seeing things from this perspective, we see that there is no one who is really bad. No one is evil in an absolute way.

Everyone does what he thinks is good. There is no bad person; there is no evil person; there is only the ignorant person.

Most of the time we don't know why we believe something; it just fits in with what we were taught. For example, many people believe that feeling emotional pain is bad for them. Some people believe that feeling anger is bad. Some believe that being lazy is good. Many people believe that being loved is a wonderful thing. But how do you know it is a good thing for you? You don't really know if something is good until you investigate and find out for yourself.

You hear psychologists and teachers tell you that the best thing to do is to know yourself, or to be enlightened. And you say, "Yes, this is a good thing." But how do you know? You don't, really. You might go ahead and do whatever they suggest, like doing twenty years of yoga because you believe that that will lead you to what is good.

So there you are, doing weird things like standing on your head for two hours a day, putting your leg around your neck, doing all kinds of contortions. People might look at you and wonder why you're putting yourself through all that. But clearly you're doing it because you believe it's the good thing for you to do. You don't think you're crazy.

You may actually be right about what you're doing; it may be leading you to what is the good. But you need to investigate, not act on what someone else has told you.

It is curious that although knowledge is such a basic thing for humans—something we use all the time and that we depend on every second for our existence—most of us go through school for years, and no one ever tells us how knowledge is important in a real way. We are taught economics so we can make money, or we learn chemistry so we can become a chemist. We need to learn literature so that we can enjoy reading, history to have an historical perspective, art and music to appreciate culture, but we are taught nothing about thinking for ourselves. Because knowledge is not appreciated for its fundamental function, its value is not seen. We tend to value compartmentalized knowledge, which is seen as useful for certain things.

Knowledge isn't just a tool to get a good job or impress people with your erudition: it is imbedded in life itself. And knowledge is not a luxury, although many people think it is. It is as basic as air, as basic as sunlight. Every minute of our existence. It is involved in the working of our minds, in our emotional choices, and in emotional reactions.

What is the good in life? What should we really go after? No one ever thinks it is important to explore these questions, at least not important enough to look at in school or with our parents.

Before we went to school, we absorbed what our parents thought was good, and that usually is what we think is good now and is what we embody. We never even considered it; we just embodied it. We didn't ask ourselves, "Is this person who's teaching me happy? Does he have the good in his life?" If we are able to question, we can ask, "Why am I listening to these people? So what if I learn economics, physics? How many physicists are happy with their lives?" We hear that it's a good thing to be important, for example, to be a congressman or a senator. This might be true, but we don't know. We need to question: is it really true? Is it the supreme good?

The education most of us get about knowledge is not complete. There are some basic forms of knowledge that we never get or even hear about, so we don't think about whether they exist or are valuable. If we never question, how are we going to find out what is good for us?

Our work can be seen as a kind of education, or a re-examination of our knowledge, or of what we believe to be our knowledge. We usually value knowledge to a certain extent, but we fail to value it in a complete way. We know that we need knowledge, for instance, to be a doctor. But after you are a doctor, what is beyond that? Is there some other kind of knowledge that will make you a more fulfilled doctor?

Now we have seen three points. The first point is that we usually attempt to go after what we believe to be good. Second, what we believe to be good depends upon our knowledge of what we think is good. And third, our education doesn't give us a complete perspective on the value of knowledge: we are taught to restrict it to certain areas and to limit its value.

So you see, it is not a luxury to be a philosopher. A philosopher is someone who is interested in knowledge; and to be interested in knowledge is basic to happiness. If you are only an engineer, and not a philosopher as well, you will probably not be happy. You will be unhappy because many of the assumptions you are living by are not true.

Most people think of knowledge as information or know-how, such as knowing how to fix a car or how to make money, and stay occupied with it at that level most of the time. But this is another bastardization of the idea of knowledge. It is true that knowledge includes such information, but this is such a tiny, insignificant part of it.

If you are a philosopher, if you want truth, you have to question the most fundamental assumptions in your life. Suppose, for example, a squirrel believes it's a cat: will the actions of that squirrel lead it to self-fulfillment? It is going to go after the things a cat wants, and then it will complain of indigestion; "Fish doesn't sit well in my stomach." So it goes to the doctor—the cat doctor!—and gets all kinds of medicines, but of course they don't work very well. They might help a little, but the real problem is that the squirrel is eating fish because it thinks it's a cat.

If we don't know who we actually are, we are in the same situation as the squirrel. If we are in reality a certain form of life, but we believe we are something different, then we look for the knowledge and the food for that something different. This is a very basic thing.

If you feel you are a little child, you will always look for someone to take care of you. You will always be trying to fill the needs of a little child. A child needs attention, needs to be taken care of, to be protected; a child can't do certain things. How many people do you know who actually believe and feel that they are adults at all levels? Don't most of us believe at a deep level that we are children? And if I believe at a deep level that I'm a two-year-old child, what am I going to do? I'm going to look for my mother everywhere.

If you believe you are a child, you are going to behave in ways that will fulfill childish needs. You might not even be aware that you believe you are a child, since when you look in the mirror you see an adult. But when your wife looks at another man, you freak out. It seems like a matter of life and death. You go trembling to your bed. That's what a two-year-old child feels, "Mommy likes some other kid and doesn't like me; she'll probably throw me out." It sounds funny, but it's the basis of how we act a lot of the time.

It goes deeper than this. It's not only that we believe we are children when we are not and therefore take childish actions, we also become identified with what we feel and what we do. For example, many people feel that they are strong and have no weaknesses, and they believe weakness is bad. If you are identified with your strength, you will act accordingly. The belief that you are a strong person who must not experience weakness might extend into the further belief that softness and even love and gentleness are weaknesses. Then being strong means you don't experience gentleness, softness, and love. What if it is not true that you are a strong person who must not experience weakness? What if who you really are has nothing to do with strength or weakness at all? These feelings and capacities are what you feel, not who you are. You are limiting your experience with this belief, and in order to live fully and experience all of your capacities, you must explore this belief and understand it. How did you come to believe that you are a strong person who must not feel weakness? And if this is not who you are, who are you?

If I believe I'm a strong person who must not feel weakness, I'm going to choose certain kinds of friends and do certain kinds of activities, do certain kinds of jobs, dress in certain clothes, drive a certain kind of car, and so on. But if I find out that I'm not the person who is strong and must not feel weakness, I may discover that I can also feel weaknesses, as well as all kinds of other feelings, and that none of them define me. Then my choice of friends, jobs, career, spouse, what I wear and drive might be different. My choices might correspond more to who I really am. I will get what I actually want, and not just satisfy an image or idea of myself that exists only in my mind.

We see that it is not only a matter of what is good for you, but of who or what you take yourself to be. How do you know what is good for you if you don't know who you are? If you think you are someone who was born on a certain date, who grew up and is going to die, you are limiting yourself. What if you have a body that was born and that will die one day but you are something beyond that body? Don't you think you will see then that you have different needs? Won't you see that what you believe are your needs are really the needs of your body and not *your* needs?

Yes, the body needs this and that, but I myself, I don't really need these things. I need other kinds of things. How are you going to be happy if you believe that the needs of your body are your needs? Your body might be satisfied, but you will always feel miserable. You will feel, "I don't have what I want; I'm comfortable, I've got satin sheets, bubble baths, massages, nice sex, a comfortable car, I live in a nice house. All these things seem to be fine, but I keep getting sick." Why? Because there's a part of you that's not getting what it needs.

If you don't find out who you are, how are you ever going to know if the life you live is the life you really want?

We have all kinds of feelings, emotions, reactions, preferences, and prejudices that we take for granted and try to live by. They are based on knowledge which we take for granted, but which very well might be erroneous. For instance, fear is one of the emotions that most people find unpleasant and want to get rid of. But we are afraid of something only if we believe it is a danger to us. What we feel is dangerous to us depends on what we take ourselves to be: if we think we are two years old, many things are going to feel dangerous to us which really aren't.

Remember, I'm not giving you knowledge; I'm questioning the issue of knowledge. We're investigating knowledge itself. You don't need to accept or reject what I'm saying. The point is to investigate. It's for everyone to find out for themselves, to confront what you take yourself to be. If you take yourself to be a child, you'll be scared of many things: scared to be alone, to do new things, go to new places, and take risks. If you take yourself to be your mind, you'll be scared of your thoughts stopping, terrified if your mind gets quiet. So you'll always be thinking, wanting to keep it going. If you think you are your body, you will do everything to avoid death, which usually means you avoid living.

Fear is dependent on what we think we are. My experience is that most of the things people find frightening are scary because of ignorance. People are scared of anger, of sadness, they're scared of love, they're scared of independence, they're scared of dependence, they're scared of compassion, they're scared of emptiness, they're scared of all kinds of things. Why? Because they don't know; they don't have right knowledge of these things.

Some people are scared of aloneness, some are scared of feeling big, some are scared of feeling happy, and some are scared of feeling scared. They think these are bad things to feel because what they think they know about them makes them seem dangerous.

What if you investigate and find out that what you are cannot be destroyed? Am I really a person who has such and such a quality? Am I my thoughts, my mind? Am I really the body that is sitting here? When you investigate, you will probably see that although these things exist, you are something beyond these things and you might see that what is beyond these things can't be harmed. Maybe if you investigate, one of these days you will find out that you are something which can't be harmed or changed or influenced, and never dies. Then what could frighten you?

You are scared of death only because you believe that you are something that can die. You are scared of death when you believe you are your body, and you think, "When the body dies, God, what will happen?" You believe you'll lose everything. But if you realize that you really are something deeper and more basic than your body, then death might be interesting, a new experience. It could be experienced as exciting. It depends on your knowledge.

Knowledge also extends to feelings. If you are sad, how do you know it? Are you thinking that you are sad? Is that how you know? Do you look at your face in the mirror and see tears, and think, "Oh, that means I'm sad"? How do you know when you are angry? This is a form of knowledge, and it can extend to very subtle levels. And there are forms of knowing even beyond the level of feeling. When I talk about self-knowledge, knowing who you are, I'm not talking about anything you can read in a book, or anything anyone else can teach you. I mean knowledge that comes from your own experience—a felt kind of knowledge. When we say that someone is sensitive we mean that person has this felt knowledge.

We say others are thick-skinned or calloused, which means that they can't feel much and don't know what they feel.

So we return to our original topic: what is knowledge and what is its importance to us? How does that apply to us here? Here we are learning to gain and appreciate the knowledge we need to find what is good for our lives. So we investigate our desires, fears, and feelings in terms of where they come from, what they mean, what we take ourselves to be in experiencing each one, leading to finally knowing who we are. The more we gain knowledge of who we are, the more our desires for what we think is good for us will change and reflect reality, become objective. And the more our belief about what is good corresponds to what we actually are, the better chance there is to be fulfilled, to live in harmony and peace.

So whenever we have an issue, a conflict, any problem or difficulty, it is good to ask ourselves, "What am I assuming that I know?" "Is there something that I think I know that I really don't know?" If you are acting in a certain way and you see it leading to negative results, you need to find out what assumptions and beliefs you are acting on. Remember the premise we established that we always do what we think is best—what is the good in the moment—and that the beliefs on which we base our choices are often unconscious. When you see the belief behind your actions, check it out. Is it true? Is your knowledge correct?

If you investigate what you believe you know, if you investigate the basis of all your knowledge and all your feelings, you may discover that there is more to you than you ever suspected, parts of you that no one ever told you about. When you discover these aspects of yourself, they will change what you want, what you think is good for you, what you think is the best way to live your life, how you live your life, and even what you believe life is for.

What if I told you that what a person usually believes himself to be is actually one millionth of what he actually is?

What if what most people take themselves to be is like the dry skin of an onion compared to the onion itself? How can someone who's taking that dry shell to be the totality of himself live correctly? How can he know what is right and not right for himself?

When you know that you are something beyond your body, mind, emotions, sensations, that there is a lot more to you which is deeper than these things, your point of view about life will change. If all your life you've looked for somebody to love you, and then find that your nature is love, what will happen to that search? You spent all of your life trying to get love, and then realize that you are love; you are no longer the bee looking for nectar; you are the flower itself. Suddenly your perspective is totally shifted; now there will be something else to do with your life other than searching for love.

To work on gaining knowledge about ourselves, we use every possible means: emotional methods, energetic methods, psychological methods. We need to sharpen our capacity to learn, our ability to investigate, to see, to understand, and to know. We need to learn how to learn. Then we can go on finding out who we are, what's really there, what life is about, what is really good, what we are supposed to go after.

We might ask whether it is good to go after the good at all. We might find out, when we discover what is really the good, the ultimate good, the supreme good, for instance, that it is a quality of the supreme that you don't go after.

There are other ways to find the good than trying to find it, but we tend to pursue it because that is the only way we know. When you know that something is good, you go after it any way you can.

You may find out that you need to pursue the good by not pursuing it at all. You need to suspend what you believe to be true, not throw it away but to suspect your knowledge. By questioning and investigating it, you will be able to sift through what you think you know and with an open mind allow other kinds of perceptions and values and even actions to emerge in you. As your perspective widens the picture is bigger and your ability to know increases.

S: Is awareness part of investigating?

AH: Clearly, knowledge requires awareness; without awareness you can't know yourself. You don't know you are sad unless you are aware of the sensations in your body. Many people are sad and don't realize it because most of the time they aren't aware of their bodies. They are thinking, so there's a whirlwind or storm going through their minds trying to figure out or apply what they know.

When there is more awareness in the body, the capacity to know feelings increases. Knowledge requires awareness more than anything else, but it also requires discrimination, strength, patience, courage, kindness, gentleness with oneself, perseverance, and humor. Our technical knowledge here encourages these innate qualities. In a sense you could say that what we do here is to supplement the education that we get elsewhere. We start with exercises, to foster our awareness, and then our awareness leads to knowledge. Our work can be seen as freeing our capacity to know. When we become more open and curious about knowledge, we come upon even more basic knowledge. Our experience of our essential nature becomes a kind of knowledge that is more intimate and precise than we have been used to. This opens us up to realms of knowledge we had not imagined existed.

Here, experience and knowledge become inseparable; experience is knowledge. The greater knowledge that becomes available through the experience of Essence can develop and deepen to the extent of recognizing that we are knowledge. Our bodies and minds *are* knowledge. Even our environment turns out to be knowledge.

This happens when Essence reveals its boundless dimensions. At this level of experience we find a knowledge that is not information, but a knowledge that is all experience. Here we see that all perception, all experience, all of existence is nothing but knowledge. This deeper knowledge becomes available when we start seeing that all experience and all that exists is knowledge, a knowledge that is itself presence, is Being.

This is sometimes referred to in religious language as God's knowledge or God's mind. It is simply seeing that all of existence, both in ourselves and in the universe, is in some fundamental way, Being. Then the universe is nothing but the self-existing conceptual patterning of this boundless and mysterious Being.

Then it is possible to see that Being itself is knowledge, knowledge that is not a content of our minds, but rather is the ground for it, as well as for the universe in its entirety. We recognize here that this Being is not only patterned as knowledge which makes up the totality of existence, but that Being in its purity is a knowingness, a consciousness, an awareness. It is both knowledge and knowing. It is the knower and the known. It is both the presence of knowledge and the capacity for knowing, which is implicit in all knowledge.

This ultimate knowledge reveals itself also to be the ultimate good, for it is both our essential nature and the nature of everything. It makes us see that everything is available, and that everything is ultimately good in a realm beyond the dichotomy of good and bad.

However, for us to arrive at such ultimate knowledge, we need to start by appreciating knowledge at whatever level of understanding we are living our lives. When we have this real and open appreciation of knowledge, it can reveal to us its true and ultimate nature; it can reveal to us not only the relative and transitory good, but also the ultimate good, the supreme good.

ELEVEN

Being and Understanding

A.H. Almaas: So, today I will answer questions.

Student: Will you talk about the process of understanding?

AH: Okay. The human potential for understanding is both a curse and a possibility for great fulfillment. A being without a mind, like an animal or a tree, does not need understanding. As a result, such a being does not have much suffering, and no mental suffering. At the same time, there is no creativity, no unfoldment. The experience doesn't change much from one day to the next. But because we have minds, it is possible for us to have understanding, which adds a whole dimension to our existence. The presence of the mind, and with it understanding, is both the cause of our suffering, and the possibility for us to experience ourselves deeply, expansively, and creatively.

The moment we have a mind, understanding becomes imperative, since without understanding suffering would simply continue. When you have a mind, it becomes natural to have ideas about things and about yourself. You take yourself to be a certain someone or a certain thing. You have memory, from which you create images of who you are, and because of this you develop fears and desires. Without memory, there would be no fears and no desires.

So the mind makes possible many human attributes that other creatures on earth do not share. We have memory, we have conceptualization and thinking processes; along with these come emotional development, a sense of identity, a world view, a perspective on reality. These relate directly to the mind, which registers all our thoughts and experiences as memories. These memories then determine what we expect, how we look at reality, what we think we are and what we think we need.

And you probably know from self-observation, this is the cause of our suffering. If you didn't remember past bad times, you wouldn't be frightened now; and if you didn't recall the good times, you would have no desires and longings. Without the capacity for remembering, there would be no suffering. You'd be like a contented tree or animal.

These elements of the mind—memory, conceptualization, thinking processes, creation of images, projections into the future, and so forth—become the basic ingredients of our suffering. Ideas and experiences from the past, from early childhood as well as later on, good and bad, form the foundation of your assumptions about who you are. For example, if as a youngster your mother always thinks you're cute, you'll build up an idea that you're a cute person. If she thinks you're dumb, you'll build up an idea that you're dumb. If, for whatever reason, you always feel weak with your father, you'll build up an idea that you're a weak person. Not only that, both your mother and father think you're a person, so you build up an idea that you're a person. Right? It is very basic. Your mother talks to you as a child in a body; who's she talking to? You look at your body and decide that it's you.

Your mind holds on to these childhood happenings and stores them in its memory. They become the building blocks of what you think you are, and then you're stuck with them. If you're a weak person, you're always going to be a weak person. If you believe that you must be tough, you will always get stuck being tough, even when you don't have to be, even when something nice is happening. You can't stop it. Your mind is stuck on thinking you're tough, and it can't change.

What understanding gives us is the possibility of actually seeing through this process. Without understanding, you'll just identify with these old self-images and go on believing that you're a person who has such and such a quality, who is weak or dumb, who eats too much or gets taken advantage of, or feels nervous at parties, and so forth. Self-image upon self-image. And you'll go on like that for the rest of your life, which is what most people do.

Now, understanding offers the possibility of seeing that you're taking yourself to be a certain self-image. Then you can start to ask yourself why. A person who has grown up thinking, "I'm a jerk" or "I'm a bitch," now begins to question the idea. "I seem to behave like a jerk, and deep down I think I am, but why?" "When people talk to me I often respond as if I'm a bitch, but why? Why do I still believe it about myself?"

If you don't try to use your understanding to investigate these self-concepts, it means you like your life just fine with them as they are. If you use your understanding, you notice that not everyone behaves like a jerk, but you do. If you investigate, if you let yourself be open and curious about it, you'll find out what is happening. You'll discover that your father was a jerk, and you liked him and wanted to be like him. What's more, you liked your mother very much and she liked your father, so you figured, "I'll be a jerk like my father and then they'll both like me." Most of the time, this kind of decision is completely unconscious. You go around being a jerk, even though everyone gives you a hard time about it, because it helps you feel that mommy and daddy are always there liking you.

Now, if you use the point of view of understanding, you can get to the origin of this pattern. "I believe I'm a jerk and continue believing it, because that way my mommy and daddy like me, and I feel lovable." When you see this, you see how that part of the personality was created. You see that it's unnecessary now, in present time, because not everyone who matters to you now likes jerks. Maybe your mother liked your father that way, but not everyone is like that.

Of course, the process of understanding can go deeper. You might wonder, "What's this big deal about people liking me? Why do I want people to like me? I always wanted to be a jerk because I thought then people would like me. Now I discover that they don't necessarily like me that way at all, so I'll immediately try to find a new way to behave so that they will." You decide that the best way to do this is to become self-realized. So, why do you want to be self-realized? Because you want people to like you. You *still* want people to like you. And if you pursue understanding, you investigate the issue.

If you didn't seek understanding, you'd just go around trying to make people like you, which is what most people do. But if you apply understanding, in time you'll see why you do that, and you'll see not only that it doesn't work, but that it's not necessary for your happiness. It's utterly superfluous and not what you deeply want to pursue. So, this shows us something about the usefulness of understanding.

However, understanding is also something much deeper. We've just seen how it reveals the falsehood, but we have not yet seen how it reveals the truth: understanding reveals what you are not, and what you are. You see that you're not actually a jerk. But then you wonder, "What am I if I'm not a jerk? Maybe I'm a good, loving person." Okay, so you become a loving person. Then after a while you begin to investigate yourself again, not according to whether you're a jerky person or a loving person, but in terms of whether you're a person at all. When you begin to investigate self-image at this level, you begin getting closer to the truth. You start seeing that the notion of a person is another idea formulated by the mind. But the idea of a person is not something you learned only from your parents; it's human conditioning.

However, our deepest nature is not that of a person. We can manifest as a person, but at the deepest level, we are something that is the source of the person. When we come to the understanding that reveals the truth rather than the falsehood, then it is functioning more as a process of unfoldment. Then understanding, which has seemed to be the equivalent of looking at something objectively, is no longer separate from the process of unfoldment itself. Seeing one layer of our reality and understanding it, is the same thing as that layer coming out, unfolding like a flower opening up. Understanding becomes the same thing as the process of actually living your unfoldment. Because you understand your experience of joy, for instance, you experience yourself as joy. You become light, happy and joyous; you start joking and become bubbly and can't stop laughing. What does understanding mean then? Part of it, which is revealing the falsehood, sees whatever barrier stopped you from being joy. Then you understand what it is to be joy. To understand what it is to be joy means to be joy consciously, means to actually feel it as your very atoms.

At that level, understanding becomes clear, or you begin seeing what it is: Being and awareness of Being at the same time. Being is our true nature, right? Essence is Being. So you're being whatever aspect of Essence is arising, like joy. There is awareness, there is consciousness of that Being, which is different from the way a child perceives. A child doesn't have understanding. A child has Being, but a child isn't conscious of that Being. The child is happy, but doesn't know that it's happy, doesn't consciously feel it. Happiness is expressed, but not consciously experienced. You can tell that the child is happy, or the child is contented or peaceful, but the child's mind is not conscious of it.

Understanding, then, includes the mind becoming an expression or a channel for Being. Mind becomes connected to Being, not separate from it like it was when you were a child, or like it was when you were an adult just seeing your issues. At this level understanding becomes the unity, the interface, the meeting of Being and mind. You are Being, but there is also awareness of the beingness. This consciousness of beingness is understanding.

So, then you might say that you understand yourself. But this is not a description of who you are. It's not the understanding. Understanding is not "I am such and such. I am joy." A statement is not understanding. Understanding is the actual embodiment of the state, the insightful beingness of it. Understanding is the unity of Being and insight. Understanding love, then, doesn't mean knowing love is this or that, love is good, love is sweet, love affects you in this warm way, love nourishes you. Understanding love is to be love in the moment, to feel what it's like. If you understand this completely, which means that you are completely and totally love, with a discriminating consciousness of the state, understanding automatically moves the state to a deeper level. The moment there is completeness in that state, the insight is there—insight is the union of your mind and your Being at that moment.

This is love. And you always know it, though sometimes you may not be able to say what it is. The moment this happens, there is no compulsion to continue experiencing yourself as love; only if it is objectively needed will it arise. The next thing just arises. This is the unfoldment.

S: Is that what you mean when you talk about unfoldment of a state leading to a station?

AH: Yes. You achieve a station when you've worked through the issues about an aspect of Essence, so that you have the objective understanding of what that aspect is. Of course, the process is very rich, with many modes and dimensions. It's not as if you realize love, you understand it and then you're done. It's much larger and richer. When you understand something completely, you go to the next level of your being. If you don't understand it, you get to stay where you are.

So understanding is a development which also brings loss. The moment you understand the state you have, you lose it. Because of this, many people aren't attracted to the path of understanding. They like devotional methods and other such practices, because in them you get to develop love or compassion and keep it. You might be always feeling loving, but not know consciously what love is, what it does. When you understand love, you understand that losing it doesn't mean you don't experience it any more, but rather that love will arise in your experience only if your environment needs it. For example, the experience of compassion or love is not something I feel all the time. But if I'm working with someone and that person needs love, I experience love. If the person doesn't need love, I don't experience love, I experience something else. That's what it means for a state to become a station. It means you completely own that state. And it becomes like anything else that's really yours. You don't have to feel it all the time, because you know it is there whenever you need it.

For instance, if you're learning to cook a certain dish, you have to think about it and practice it. But when you really get to know it well, it becomes less of a concern. When it is time to cook, you cook it, and it comes out fine. Good! But there isn't that much investment in it, not much focus on cooking it better, reading books, showing it to people. The moment you really know it, it's both gone and it's yours; it's finished as a matter of concern. It's available to you, and so you go on to the next thing, to the next dish you want to learn to prepare. But if you haven't learned it completely, you stick around with it, trying to perfect it with a little more of this and some of that. And you have lots of investment in it, you are identified with the outcome. The moment you really know it and are satisfied with it, it loses its importance, not in terms of reality, but in terms of your mind. Your mind doesn't need to think about it any more. It's finished focusing, worrying, and obsessing. Your mind brought about the understanding, and has nothing to do with it any more.

So, understanding sees the barriers, sees the false, and reveals the truth. It brings a sense of the completion of something, completing the gestalt. Then it brings in the unfoldment. One of the frustrating aspects of our work here is that when you understand something, it seems to change to something else. People work on something and get to a certain essential state; they experience their strength, for example. It feels wonderful, powerful, strong, expansive and all that. The person wants to feel it all the time. But our method is understanding, and understanding will lead us into whatever is next for us. So if a person comes to experience his strength and completely understands it, he's likely to wake up one morning and find that it's gone. What happened? It's not there that much. Although the unfoldment might be experienced by the mind and the personality as a loss, it is really a movement forward, a movement deeper.

Understanding continues like this from one level to the next. The moment something is completed and you understand it, your mind moves to the next thing. This process of moving from one thing to another, losing one thing after another, will continue until you arrive at something you cannot understand. The only end of this process of understanding is experiencing yourself in a way that is unknowable.

When you finally experience your true identity, and you say, "Now what is this? Let me understand it," you can't. You want to see, but when your mind tries to go there, it disappears. You try again to understand this. You knock your head against the wall for a few years. "I have to understand this one." You look, and can't get any idea about it, can't get the flavor of it, or a feeling that goes with it. You almost get a feeling … it disappears.

You keep trying until your mind is convinced that your ultimate identity is something that cannot be known through understanding, that understanding can't reach it. And then the final realization, the final understanding is that you reach the end of understanding, the death of understanding, when finally you know that you are un-understandable. When you reach the un-understandable, that is the end of understanding. And of course, it can't be lost, because you can't understand it. If you understand it, you lose it, but that fact cannot be understood completely. By its very nature it has nothing to do with your mind. The mind has led you there, but the mind cannot go there. We can call this the death of understanding, or we can call it total understanding. Both mean the same here.

So, as you see, understanding is very curious. If you use it correctly, it will take you through the whole unfoldment process, one layer after another, until you reach a place where understanding can't go. And if you're faithful to understanding, then you cannot but reach its end. Understanding is complete when it annihilates itself. When it dies, then the mind dies, too. There is just Being, Being with no mind. You become like an animal but with the understanding that you are not understandable and the knowledge that you are that which is unknowable.

The moment you change, there is a shift from one state to another, and implicit in this is the possibility of understanding and differentiation, which are at the beginning of mind. But if this understanding can lead you to the unknowable, which is the undying and the unchangeable, then you are free to live life without fear.

When you know that you are unknowable, you know you cannot be any image, you cannot be your body or your personality, you cannot be what your mother thought you were or what your father said you were; you cannot be rejected or hurt, you cannot die or be afraid because anything that can die is knowable. What can die? The body can die. What can be hurt? Your ideas about yourself, your self-image? But when you know that you are not knowable, how can anybody hurt or reject you? How can anyone do anything to you?

Even your own mind can't hurt you. How can you criticize yourself? What's there to criticize? But as long as you have ideas about who you are, you will have ideas about how you should be, and criticize yourself: you should be bigger, smaller, smarter, better looking.

But when you reach the place of understanding, your mind asks, "What is this?" and the only answer is "Beats me." You honestly don't know. So you can't give yourself a hard time. You don't know because you cannot be known. That's freedom, then.

When you can't pinpoint yourself with your mind, then you're free. Nothing can happen to you. You're beyond the concepts of the mind. You're beyond the concepts of pain and pleasure, life and death, big and small, good and bad. It is the final understanding, the final knowledge and fruit of knowledge to know that you are not knowable.

In some traditions, one of the names for understanding is "the angel of revelation." It is that which reveals. It continues revealing, continues revealing, continues revealing. And it is said that the angel of revelation cannot be in the presence of God. It leads you all the way there, but it cannot enter—nobody and nothing can enter. It reveals the road, completely, one step after another, until you get to the source, and then the angel of revelation disappears. Then there is no understanding, there is just Being, which we can call total understanding.

The unfoldment of all the levels and manifestations is really what is beautiful. It is the expression of beauty, grace, differentiation—all the colors and varied forms. That is life. Without that, there is no life, you just go to the beyond, the unknowable, and you don't need to be a human being. You're just being without knowing.

So, understanding is linked with human life. Life is itself a process of unfoldment; it is the living of the unfoldment. Life is not the final repose in the unknowable identity. That's not life, that's beyond life. You could be dead, and there would be no difference. Because the unknowable doesn't change, and you know that it is you, you know you cannot die. When you know absolutely that it is you that does not change, does not die, then there is freedom. There is release from fear. You experience the multiplicity of creation in life—all the beauty of it. Then the life, which is the personal life, becomes fulfilled. And understanding is the same thing as living that life.

When you understand what it's all about, what this life is about, why we are here—when you understand who you are and why you're here—you understand the meaning, in a sense, of everything. Everything is then meaningful, everything has an innate, deep sense to it that is absolute and central. So it's not a life of strife, but rather of unfoldment, and unfoldment is inherently fulfilling. Understanding is not only a process that functions to take you from one place to another, but also is in itself the actual living of the unfold-ment. And through the process you come to understand the place of suffering, of difficulty, and of personality in the whole scheme. You live what is called the conscious life: you regain your being just as it was when you were an infant, but it's conscious now.

Without mind, there is no variety, discrimination or dif-ferentiation; we see no form and hence, no beauty. Mind is the creator of form, the creator of beauty, and understanding is that process of creation, of unfoldment. So, the fulfillment of our life is to see life objectively, to see what's really there. To know, for example, that life is the expression and fulfill-ment and celebration of beauty. This is what we are here for. We're not here for anything else.

Everyone wants this life of fulfillment, beauty and har-mony, but most people want to reach it without going through the process of understanding. They want it to come from someone else through some magical transmission. They don't want to do it by understanding. But the process is understanding, and can happen in no other way.

S: Since we are the result of our conditioning, and since the human condition is a concept, how do we know that our understanding is not based upon our conditioning or our concepts? Where does the capacity to understand reality come from? If the understanding is within the human frame-work of being conditioned, isn't it still bound by our mis-conceptions?

AH: Yes, the understanding is bound, that's true, but it's more subtle than that. It's true that for understanding to occur there must be concepts and differentiation. The world of concepts, the world of personality and mind, is ultimately conceptual, but it's not real. I call it the dream world. The dream world is not chaotic, however. There is an order to it. It's an ordered fake reality, an ordered dream world. And understanding can follow that order, going through the depths and levels of it.

Understanding is the expression of the ultimate reality in this world. The intelligence that is actually producing understanding is the unknowable, which, when it encounters concepts, disintegrates them one after another. This disintegration, or erasing of concepts as they come up against the unknowable, is the process of understanding. When mind and Being make contact, the particular concept at hand is integrated, or metabolized, into Being. That's why you go to the next level, the next concept.

It's true that the world of the mind, of concepts, is not the truest reality. But understanding is the meeting of that unreal world with the completely real. Understanding itself is neither wholly real or unreal; it is a meeting of the two. The meeting is a transformation, and the transformation is understanding.

So understanding happens only when what is completely real in you—the unknowable, your final identity—is in contact with your concepts, with your mind. The process is one of disintegration of concepts. Isn't that what happens when you understand? You have a certain concept, see through it and then it dissolves. Being comes in contact with mind. This is what we experience as insight. Then there is completion of that level and you move on to the next. If Being doesn't come in contact with the mind, there is no real insight, only mental knowledge. And because mental knowledge is not real understanding, there is no transformation. The concept is not burned up and dissolved into Being. The person simply goes from one part of the concept to another; it's just a matter of mental rearrangement.

So, while we could say that from an absolute perspective understanding is not real, it does have an order, a depth that can be explored. An alternative way of saying this is that understanding, especially on the essential level, is simply the true discrimination of the unfoldment of Being. So understanding is ultimately real, for it is the revelation of the mysteries of Being. The concepts get wider and bigger as you go deeper. Concepts, you have to understand, are not intrinsically bad. You need concepts to function. You need the concept of a table in order to use one. Right? You need the concept of a car if you want to drive one.

Concepts are useful, but they trap you if you forget that they are concepts, if you take them to be the actual reality. And of course, the most difficult, ensnaring trap is to take your concepts of yourself to be who you really are. If you believe the concept of the car is the actual car, you won't be seeing reality completely clearly, but it's not going to hurt you. Right? But if you take your concept of yourself as you, that's when your problems start.

When you understand the unknowable, you can understand the nature of concepts and how they can be used. Concepts are seen as neutral. Like many other things, how concepts are used determines the nature of their effect. You can be restricted by concepts, or you can use them intelligently, expanding them from smaller to bigger and bigger ones, until the concept becomes so big that it has no boundaries, and ceases being a concept. That then is the unknowable.

Concepts enable us to reach understanding. Understanding is nothing but the understanding of concepts. But ultimately, everything is concepts, and hence understanding is the true revelation of everything. The essential aspect that functions as understanding, which we sometimes call the "diamond consciousness," is a manifestation of the absolute reality. Out of Being arises the capacity for understanding, for the encounter between absolute reality and the conceptual reality of the mind.

At a deeper level of realization there is a union, a co-emergence, of the absolute reality and the diamond consciousness. At this level, understanding is the flow of reality, the unfoldment of the beingness of the absolute in its richness and color.

S: So what is it that's different between the part of Essence that is the diamond consciousness and the part that's unknowable? You just said that the diamond consciousness is a manifestation. Is it a concept?

AH: Ultimately, yes. But it is a concept only from the perspective of the unknowable, not from other levels. From other levels, it's real and concrete. At its own level it is true, absolute. Its intelligence is the absolute reality, Being itself. It is Being. All Essence is Being, it's important to remember that. And the diamond consciousness is an aspect of Essence. It's Being, but Being with form.

S: By absolute reality, I assume you mean the truth. And how can one know the ultimate truth?

AH: That's what I have been saying—you can't know it.

S: If you can't know it, how can you ever get there?

AH: Well, when I say you can't know it, that doesn't mean you cannot be it. You can know it as not-knowing. See, we think of knowing only in terms of concepts. That's why I say you cannot know it, because you can't conceptualize it. You can't know it in the sense that you cannot identify or name it. Your mind cannot look at it, but your mind knows it's there by the mere fact that when it approaches the absolute reality, the mind disappears. When you experience absolute reality directly, your mind doesn't know what happened. In fact, the mind is incapable of conceptualizing absolute reality at all, the mind can't even recall the experience. After you encounter absolute reality directly, after a while your mind will ask, "What happened? I don't remember what happened!" And you won't end up with any conceptual knowledge. Why? Because absolute reality is the experience of unity. The moment the mind looks at absolute reality, it becomes that reality. The separation implicit in one thing looking at another dissolves.

This is a certain kind of knowledge, but it is not knowledge in the way we usually think of it. It's knowledge by being. You simply are the reality. The mind can know it only indirectly. It knows the reality exists because it knows there's something there that it cannot know. Ultimately, the mind also knows that its very nature is that of reality, because the moment it sees that reality is unknowable, it also perceives the absence of duality. This means that there is absolute unity, there are not two; the mind and absolute reality are one.

It's attainable in the sense that you realize what I've been describing: at some point the mind sees that there is such a thing as absolute reality. This happens when you reach the limit of understanding who you are, which is the limit of understanding. You also see that reality has always been there; it has always been the nature of things. So, it is attainable in the sense that you know, "Yeah! That's me, I've always been that."

The mind then becomes reality. Actually, the mind has always been reality; it is in a state of "becoming" only at the moment of recognition. In that instant, the mind is enlightened and knows its true nature. Its nature is nothing graspable.

Now, as you listen to me, it's very hard to grasp this idea because the mind functions by having concepts it can hold on to. As the mind understands more and more, it reaches a place where it knows that not everything can be known conceptually. It knows definitely, absolutely, that something is there, but the mind, itself, cannot know it. Beingness, however, knows itself, and knows itself not by a reflection on itself, but just by being it. If I'm being myself, and I want to find out what I'm being, I can't exactly tell. But I know I'm being myself. The closest way to describe it is to say, "It's like nothing."

But it's not exactly like nothing, because there's a sense of being, a sense of reality and of truth. The mind cannot say it is this or that, and capture it conceptually. It tries! My mind does that; its tendency is to look for a way to identify the self. It might say, "I see, it's just an expansive clarity, everything's clear, that's me." And then the mind's happy. But when I look deeper, I see that wasn't who I am, that was clarity, one of the manifestations of me. Clarity is a concept. When I see through that, the mind disappears. Then the mind gets trickier, it thinks, "Oh, I am just nothing," and I go around believing, "I have no self, I am nothing." My mind is happy, thinking, "Oh, I found it, I'm nothing." I may actually experience myself as this nothingness, but if my mind really looks deeper, something will happen of its own accord, and I'll see that even the nothing is not yet who I am.

The mind knows by inference, and you know it directly, because it is you. You know in the sense of being, not in the sense of reflection, not in the sense of having qualities. So, when we say absolute, we mean Being—Essence with no qualities, before qualities come into Being. Then you know it's the source of everything, because you see everything arising from it.

S: It seems the problem is that it's attainable, but not pursuable. Because the pursuit defeats the attainment, and yet we're oriented towards the pursuit.

AH: You can pursue it and you cannot pursue it; both are true. When you know it, you see that it is possible to pursue if you have the intelligence, and the correct map. Pursuing then has a different meaning. It no longer involves effort. But, how can you pursue without exerting effort? From the perspective of the unknowable, any concept can be used to attain Being, nothing is bad. Even effort can have a place in it. And, remember, we use the word "attain," but it is not attainable. It is not attainable because it is already there.

S: So, the interference that we get, in terms of whether we accept, pursue, or attain, are those all superego restrictions?

AH: Yes, on a certain level. Superego is the internalized voice of our parents' and societies' restrictions and beliefs about how things should be. Clearly these ideas restrict our pursuit of understanding. But we are speaking today more of the functioning of concepts on a level beyond the content of any particular society's concepts. Mind is limited to working with concepts and images. If you believe in the images as reality, you're not seeing things as they are and you get into difficulty. Eventually understanding comes to know that this is what the mind does; it creates images. If you understand that they're really images, you live with them, and in time, see their beauty. The mind can create both horrible and wonderful images.

But, we're talking about understanding, and of course, everything leads to the unknowable. The process of understanding is what's important. It is the actual method of the path, it's the path itself and it's also the fruit of the path. It is life itself. Human life can be seen as understanding. It can also be seen from other perspectives, such as love or will. But, today we're looking from the perspective of understanding.

I'm saying all this so that we know that understanding is not just another little tool that we're using to get to some goodie. There are all kinds of techniques for trying to get goodies: positive affirmation, meditation, various spiritual and physical exercises. There's this tool and that technique, and then there's understanding, unique in its relationship to reality. Understanding is not a technique. Understanding is the organic process of living itself. It is the unfoldment of Being as it reveals its mystery and beauty.

One of the influences which restricts our understanding is school conditioning. We learn that understanding is mental—figuring things out, deducing, connecting information, and so forth. But this is only the beginning, the most superficial kind of understanding. True understanding means there is Being, there is Essence. When there's no Essence, there is no true understanding. I think most people here know the difference between mental understanding and true understanding. With true understanding, there's an expansion, there's depth, lightness and aliveness, arising from Being coming in contact with the mind, expanding and exploding it.

Ultimately we are that Being. Understanding brings us closer to ourselves; we're being ourselves because we are the Being that's coming in contact with the concept, with the mind. So, the process of understanding is the process of Being oneself, more and more. It's the process of actualization, the process of realization.

Understanding is like a prism. If you have pure light passing through a prism, you have different colors. They are creativity and beauty, they are the forms of light. That is the life. Without the prism, it is just light by itself, with no differentiation. You don't see anything. But through understanding, you come in time to understand the whole thing, the whole process. Nothing needs to be done; you just see. That's understanding, that's life, that's reality, that's the unknowable. You know the whole thing, not just one part.

We can see how each sector of the personality relates to one of the colors of the prism. Our method—the Diamond Approach—allows us to see this connection. One sector is connected to the red, one to the green, one to the yellow, and so on. By seeing the connections you start experiencing the colors, the aspects of Essence, which are not only color, but pure light as well.

If you know the colors of the prism, it's easier. The next step is to know light with no color, which is the unknowable. That's our approach. First you know the aspects of Essence, and then you know they are Being, they are light. But, you're still looking at the color. You see the prism itself, and you see that understanding is the prism that's creating all these colors. Then it is possible to see the actual beingness of the colors, of the aspects. You see compassion, for instance, as Being, and you say, "I am compassion, I am love." But, if you just say "I am," if you look at the "I am" quality of the aspect without looking at the compassion quality, that is the unknowable. Of course, you could say, "Oh, it's clear, or it's yellow or pink," and it would be a correct perception from a certain level. However, if you go deep into the actual nature, the essence of Essence, it is pure light with no color. It is light before its differentiation into the spectrum. And what do you say about that? It's light. What do you see? You could say it's nothing, because you don't see anything. For you to see something, it must have a reflection. But, the moment it has a reflection, it has a color—the color of its reflection. But what is the color of the light? In fact, you can't say anything, but you know it has to be there.

So, that's the method: going from the particular issue of the personality to the corresponding aspect of Essence. When you go through all the corresponding aspects, they become objectified; you see them as they are, which is the true understanding from inside the prism itself. Then you go to the nature of the aspect itself, which is Being. First you say, "I am love," then you say "I am." Before the love is the source of the love.

TWELVE

Reacting, Being and Doing

Today I would like to clarify a certain point about the distinction between personality and Being. We need to understand this as accurately as possible in order to understand the process of understanding itself, the process of work on oneself, the process of the path, and to understand the goal itself, which is really the same thing. One way we can talk about how to engage in the process from the perspective of the goal is to explore how what you're looking for is already there in the process of understanding itself.

The point I want to make is very, very subtle. We will need to understand many aspects of this question, to paint a certain picture, to begin to understand the main distinction between the functioning of personality and of your true

Being. We need the most precise discrimination, the sharpest edge possible, because this issue brings up many fears, and so we usually remain vague about it. In fact, this is an issue that tends to arouse more fear the more you achieve an accurate understanding.

What we want to explore is "doing." What does it mean to "do"? Many people have questions about doing when they begin to work on themselves. Who does what? Should I do this and not do that? What am I doing when I'm understanding? Am I doing anything? To understand doing objectively, we first have to know what Being is. And to know what Being is, we need to know what reaction is. Reaction is an activity of the personality, whereas doing is related more to Being. So we will talk first about reactivity, then about Being, and then about doing.

In discussing reactivity we will talk about some subtle, but important points involving your work on understanding yourselves. Yesterday, for instance, I talked about how you never let go, never surrender, and that you never really accept anything. When I say that you never let go you might say, "What about my experiences of surrender and acceptance and letting go?" I did not say that there was no experience of letting go, no experience of surrender. I said that YOU do not let go, YOU don't surrender, YOU don't accept, not the you that you usually think of as yourself.

So how is it that there is experience of acceptance and disidentification and letting go without you doing it? How can these experiences happen? Who does it?

Let's take these terms one by one. We'll begin with the term "disidentification." We say you need to disidentify from a certain state to be able to understand it. Many methods, such as Gurdjieff's, deal with identification and disidentification. What is disidentification really? To understand disidentification, you need to understand identification. To identify with anything, any state, means simply that your mind takes a certain state for identity. Your mind holds on to an expression, or a feeling, or a state, and uses it to define you. The mind then contracts around the state in the activity of holding on to it. This very contraction of the mind creates what we call "identity."

So identifying with something is taking a concept and saying, "That's me," or "That relates to me," or "That defines me in some way." Suppose you identify with your body. Your mind looks at your body and says, "That's me." That identification is now a contraction in the body and the mind. Now how does one go about disidentifying from this belief? Contrary to what most people think, disidentification does not mean that part of you separates from the body and says, "Oh, I am not the body." This would mean that there's a part of me that I'm pushing away. Most people think disidentification is this pushing away: "I am not that."

Actually, disidentification is simply the awareness that you believe you are your body, and the understanding that that isn't true, that you are not your body. When you understand this, the false assumption disappears and there is no more belief that you are the body.

When there is disidentification, there is no one who disidentifies. Disidentification is simply the absence of identification, the absence of the contraction, the absence of the belief. If you believe that there is a part that is pushed away, you are making it real; the mind is still holding on, contracting in that place. The mind is still restricting itself. Identification is a contraction, and disidentification is a relaxation of that contraction.

This is why when you're trying to understand an emotion, it doesn't work to try to disidentify from it. It doesn't work to try to push away, fight, or deny something you are identified with. Repeating, "That's not me, that's not me …" won't do it.

To disidentify, first you must be aware of the identification, then you must understand it. The moment that you become aware of the identification, there is the possibility of disidentification. When there is an understanding of what the identification is all about, when you explore—why you believe this about yourself, on what evidence, when you learned it—then the identification dissolves, because the identification is nothing but the absence of understanding. Then the contraction, the tension in the mind that was holding on to the identification, just dissolves.

If you assume, as most people do, that there is someone there who either is identified or not, you are assuming that disidentification is an activity, something that you do. And this is the main distinction we want to make—disidentification is not an activity. Disidentification is simply the cessation of a certain activity. The activity is in the identification, and in the believing and acting according to certain assumptions.

So we can see why disidentification can't be an activity; if it were an activity, it would not be disidentification, but identification with something else. It would be just a substitution. If there is someone who is moving away from something else, that someone must be identified with something, or at least with the desire to move away from something. True disidentification means the cessation of identification, the cessation of taking something to be you, or to belong to you, or to define you. The practice of not acting out on what you feel or believe is not disidentification. Some people take this practice to mean disidentification. In our perspective, this is a practice that can lead to disidentification.

Let's look at it in practical terms now. Suppose you are identified with anger. When the disidentification happens, there is an awareness of the anger without identification. That's all. You're not aware that there is anger there and you are not it. If that happens, that only means that the person who is looking at the anger is identified with something else.

This is why we sometimes feel that disidentification means separating from something.

Perhaps you can see now that you cannot try to disidentify. If you try to disidentify, then what you're doing is identifying with something else, so something else is saying "no" to what you're trying to disidentify from. What most people call disidentification is simply a rejection. When you try to disidentify from something, aren't you saying that this is something I shouldn't be? It is already an implicit judgment that this is no good, and you should get away from it. You are rejecting even if you think that you're doing it for understanding.

Now let's discuss another term, "surrender." What is the actual experience of surrender? What is the experience of feeling you have surrendered? Can you surrender in the sense that surrender is an activity you engage in? How do you go about surrendering? Can you say, "Now I'm not surrendering and now I'm going to surrender," as if there is somebody there who is moving from lack of surrender to surrender? Is there such a thing? Sometimes it feels as if there is. You experience a change; there is tension, and then there is a melting of tension. And you say, "Yes, this is surrender; I have surrendered." Did you surrender? Or did surrender happen? If it happened, what was the actual mechanism? What actually happened? What was your part in it?

What I am challenging, or confronting, is the belief that we have surrendered, that we do something when we surrender—"It's as if I am hard and I make myself soft, as if I do the yielding or the letting go." Do I ever do it? That is exactly the sharp edge that we want to understand. Is there such a thing, and if there isn't, what is actually happening? This is similar to our question about disidentification: Do you do it? Do you disidentify? Do you surrender? Is there anything you do, any action you take, to make either of these things happen? Is acceptance an activity of your ego? Is letting go an activity of your ego? That is the question.

I'm not asking whether there really is an experience of surrender or acceptance; of course there is, we do experience that. I'm asking, is it something that you actually do? Because if it isn't, then your belief that you actually do it is going to create misunderstanding and confusion. Understanding what actually happens may help you to work more effectively in the process of understanding yourself.

Let's investigate what surrender is. Let's take the moment of surrender and put it under the microscope. What we notice first is that there is a tension, a state of holding or contraction. What is the tension, the holding, and the contraction? When there is a tension in your mind and in your body, aren't you saying no to something? You will find out from your own experience that holding, tension and contraction are simply the resistance to the experience or the perception of a certain state or a certain truth or feeling. When you say no, there is a contraction that is a form of resistance. What else could it be?

So any state of non-surrender is a contraction, a tension, a grasping. It can take many forms and be experienced at many depths. It can be hard, like armor, so that you aren't even aware of it most of the time, or it can be softer, like a defensive attitude or resistance, or it can be dullness, non-seeing, and confusion. But at the deepest level, there is always contraction when you are rejecting something in your experience. And the contraction restricts the flow of energy. It creates a barrier that separates you from the experience that you're saying no to.

Now, how does this situation change to a state of surrender? What actually happens? Remember that personality itself is fundamentally a contraction, a restriction of your experience. The experience of contraction, the tension itself is the ego at that moment, is itself the personality. If you go very deep into the experience of your personality, you'll see that, ultimately, personality is a contraction, a restriction. If you go deeper, to the origin of the personality, you'll see that the personality begins as a defensive maneuver, as a need to defend against or resist something. At all levels, personality is a resistance to something, to some truth or some state. So any activity of the personality can only be a manifestation of resistance—a saying no, a rejection, a contraction.

So how do you go from the tension, contraction and holding on to the state of surrender? If you look at your work, when it has actually happened, what do you see? What exactly has happened? This is where we have to observe with precision and subtlety, because this is the moment we usually gloss over and don't notice. We don't usually pay attention to this process. We notice after the fact that something completely changed, but we usually don't ask why.

Let's examine closely the process that leads to a state of surrender. If you observe carefully, you will see that you first become aware of the tension. If you pay attention to the tension, you realize that the tension is a resistance, a contraction. When you realize that it's a contraction which is a resistance, you want to understand the resistance. Then, when you understand what the resistance is about, the activity of resistance ceases. This simply means that you are no longer going along with the activity of saying no. It doesn't mean that you are saying yes. It just means that you were pushing and now you have stopped pushing. But stopping this activity brings the absence of personality. If the personality stops pushing, it ceases to exist, because the very existence of the personality is a contraction, a pushing. So, when you follow this process, the part of personality which is holding a particular tension will disappear when you see no more reason to push. When you realize that the pushing is useless, you stop doing it.

This is still not exactly what is called surrender; it is what is sometimes called letting go. We sometimes think of it as the personality letting go, but even this is not accurate. The personality can't let go. It just stops pushing. And when it stops pushing, it disappears. There is no person which is letting go of something. There is no entity letting go of another object.

When you stop contracting, and stop pushing, what remains is what was there in reality. For example, if you are pushing against anger, you might be resisting it because you think that it's bad, or that you are bad if you feel it. If you realize your resistance to it you will feel the anger. When we see that this is what people call letting go, we understand that all it means is that we stopped doing something, not that we are now doing something called letting go. The letting go is a non-doing. The contraction is the activity of the personality and that is all it knows how to do: resist and defend. If you assume you are doing something called letting go, look carefully into the moment that it happens. You will see that it is actually a movement from doing into non-doing, or more accurately, a cessation of activity.

Surrender is a step further than letting go, a small step further. Letting go is ceasing the activity of resistance. When you surrender, you realize that you are pushing and resisting, and then you understand it so that you're not as interested in the resistance. And then, because you have stopped pushing, a certain essential state, a certain energy arises and begins to flow. This flow of energy of the essential state, plus the letting go, the cessation of activity, is felt as surrender.

So surrender is a meeting of the personality and Essence. Personality does its work of seeing its identification, its resistance, and its contraction. That's it's part; it can't surrender. Essence comes along and melts it. The personality can't melt on its own, but it can be melted.

It is the same with acceptance: First, you realize that you are rejecting and pushing, you see it and you don't identify with it, then there is understanding of the rejection and cessation of the rejection. And finally a certain essential state flows that is called "acceptance." It feels like a blessing, a melting, a kind of vulnerability, a kind of non-defensiveness.

It's the same with understanding. When you're understanding something, can you actually understand something fundamental about your personality without the presence of Essence? Can there be a clear awareness of what is there without the presence of Essence? In fact, the awareness itself is Essence; the clarity, the objectivity itself is Essence. As we have seen the mind itself can't go all the way in understanding. Essence must be present to infuse it with the necessary quality.

We have seen that the personality doesn't do anything in the processes of disidentification, letting go, surrender or acceptance. So what does it do? How is it different from Being in this context?

If you observe your personality at any time, in any state, you'll see that it is always active. It can't be still. The ego personality is activity and reactivity. It is always reacting to something. At the deepest level, personality *is* reactivity, and reactivity by its very nature is saying no to something. You might be saying no to a certain pain, or a certain pleasure, or a certain state, a conflict, a difficult situation, to anything. When I say reactivity, I am not referring to physical actions, which are just the grossest, outer manifestations of the personality. I'm talking about when you're meditating, or allowing yourself a moment of inner reflection. How do you experience the personality then? Can the personality be completely still?

When the personality is analyzed in its minutiae you will see the cycle of action and reaction. Originally, there is the reality of what is there, and then there is saying no to that reality. Then there is hope for another reality. Then there is desire for that other reality. Right? There is a rejection of now, a hope for something else in the future, and then a desire for it. The cycle of rejection, hope and desire all together leads to an activity, to trying to achieve what is desired. Any hope, desire, activity, or reactivity necessitates more than anything else rejection of the now. If the now is completely accepted there will not be a hope, there will not be a desire, there will not be a movement away from or toward, or any movement at all. There will be stillness, complete stillness.

Student: When you say stillness, I'm aware of the breath moving. It seems like even when there is stillness, there is movement. The body moves, the breath moves.

A.H. Almaas: Yes. By stillness I don't mean that there is no movement, physical or mental movement. I'll explain more. When I say that there is no stillness, I mean that when you observe any object of your perception, you are looking at it from a place that is either going toward or away from what you are looking at. You are either saying, "I want it," or "I don't want it." So the place that you are coming from is in constant movement; it is not still. Real stillness penetrates all the way through to the place that you are coming from, or rather, it emanates from there. It doesn't mean that there is no movement in the field of perception. It has nothing to do with whether the body is moving or not. It is your center that becomes a stillness.

The personality does nothing. When you identify with your personality, it means simply that you are coming from activity, not from stillness. And that activity always involves rejection, hope, and desire.

S: Would opinion go there?

AH: Opinion? Of course, opinion, knowledge of the past, motivates your rejection, desire, and hope. Desire and hope imply remembering something from the past, so you have an opinion about seeking it out or pushing it away. Rather than just being with what is in the present, you hope for something from the past that was better. This is hope. Hope projects something into the future from the past. These hopes are not always from your own inner experience

—maybe you remember your sister looking a certain way and you want to feel like that. If you have never known that things can be better than this, you completely accept it. What else can you do? Hope and desire always imply a memory from the past and that is what makes your opinions.

S: The same must be true of rejection.

AH: Yes. Rejection is also based on memories. Not only is there activity in going after what you hope for, but there is also activity in avoiding or rejecting something.

This pattern involves an alternation between pleasure and pain. There is something that we call pleasure and something that we call pain. From this distinction comes rejection, hope and desire. But you can see that when you're rejecting the present, you're pushing against it, you're rejecting it. That very action is a contraction. At the deepest level, that action is a frustration. The heart of contraction is always a state of frustration. And the more you reject, the more you feel the frustration. The more you feel the frustration, the more desire you have to release the frustration.

But it's a vicious cycle, as you can see. The more you reject, the more there is contraction, the more frustrated you become. Then you want to do something that will release the frustration. But you do this by hoping for something in the future and rejecting the present, which creates more frustration, which makes you hope even more to release it. So you hope some more, you push, and more frustration is created.

This cycle generates the personality, and it is the experience of the personality itself. This cycle is what we call ego activity. When you really feel it, the actual substance of the personality is a feverishness, a lack of stillness, a lack of contentment. When you feel desire, it's that frustration, too. Part of the desire that we feel is a rejection of the present and a hope for something else, which brings frustration. The very movement of the personality is frustration, and the existence of the personality is that movement. The very existence of the personality is that reactivity. It's a reaction, not a spontaneous action, which I will talk about when I discuss doing.

The personality also reacts to things in itself. First, there is the original reaction based on the pleasure-pain differentiation, which creates the cycle of rejection, hope, and desire. This in turn creates certain manifestations and behaviors. Then there is a rejection of those manifestations, and the cycle is repeated again in different areas and on different levels.

S: Where does conceptualizing oneself come in relation to hope and desire, in other words, creating a static picture?

AH: Conceptualizing oneself happens as a result of this process. Conceptualizing yourself means that you use all your experiences, good and bad, to crystallize a certain picture. And this picture is mostly based on a rejection of something you don't want, something you experience as negative or painful. One of the main purposes of the creation of identity is to resist. The conceptualization of identity is simply the crystallization of that activity into an image of a person. But the core of that image is the frustration, which I call the state or affect of negative merging. Instead of harmony, there is a jagged flow through the nervous system. This is experienced as frustration, which is suffering. Psychic suffering, mental suffering is that actual contraction, that feeling of harshness, dryness, stuckness.

Whenever we are reacting to or rejecting anything, we are identifying with that core of frustration. Of course, this core of cyclic reactivity and frustration is covered with something softer, so that usually we don't feel it. We dull it with all kinds of beliefs and ideas.

So we see that the personality is constructed of a continuous cyclic movement of reactivity. It continuously produces more of itself, more frustration and suffering. Understanding this enables us to understand the processes of disidentification, letting go, surrender, and acceptance.

Now, what can we say disidentification is? If disidentification means that I'm seeing a certain state which I want to pull away from, who is it who pulls away? It can only be the reactive core rejecting the state or experience. So attempting to disidentify in this way can only increase the frustration rather than alleviate it.

So how can you really surrender? How can you truly disidentify? Since the core of frustration is attachment, contraction, and dissatisfaction, you cannot do something which could be called disidentification. The personality can only perpetuate itself. The moment you try to do something, you're turning a wheel of action and reaction which is what we call the wheel of samsara. Perhaps to you surrender means that you will engage in an activity. But the activity of the personality is a rejection, which is ultimately hope and desire, leading to frustration. How can that be surrender?

Surrender can only be awareness of activity. When you are aware of that activity, you're not interested in engaging in it. If you can feel the core of frustration directly and understand what it is, you are not engaged in it even though you might be feeling it. And the more you see it, the more it becomes ego-alien. If you see the activity and don't go along with it, then the essential state which you've been resisting will arise, and melt away the contraction and reactivity. What arises is a kind of acceptance and love, which flows and melts you away.

It never was you, that contraction, even though you believed it was. You become melted, but it is not something you can will from within because the will of the personality is contraction.

If you look deeply at the personality functioning in the body, beyond the verbal level in your awareness, and if you're not actively acting from your frustration, you can see these strands of contractions. If you feel this very deeply, and let the tension relax without identifying, the big thick contraction dissolves and you see the very thin strands of what we call the negative merging affect itself. They are like lines, like nerves that still have a contraction, a dryness in them. And when you reach that place, you can begin to understand the activity of the personality. You will see that the moment there is some impulse in you, an intention to react, even to act to pay attention to something, you feel these strands of contraction and the effect of them. You'll feel first of all that your breathing becomes more intentional, rather than spontaneous. You'll feel that your muscles start to become tense. The action of the personality is simply those strands getting squeezed together to make a big, thick strand of tension. This is what you feel as will, as determination. This determination is a springboard for your action. The personality cannot act unless all of these strands are massed together to move from. Without that, there is nothing. There is an emptiness you can't jump from.

The feeling of negative merging or the tiny strands of contraction are felt as harshness, as if there were sand on the nerves, a prickliness. That is the contraction when it is felt on the deepest level, and is not covered by the level which is felt as a smoothing out or as dullness. And the moment you want to do something, the moment there is the slightest ego intention, the subtlest activity, it brings these tiny strands together, increasing the tension, compacting them. As they are compacted, more of that contraction results. So after a while you have a big tension somewhere in your body, and from this you react. Without this tension, you cannot take any ego action. This is because there is actually nothing underneath the ego. So the ego has to amass this contraction in order to take action. The solid contraction is a springboard for the activity of ego. This is where you come from when you act from personality: a solidification and intensification of the contraction that is already there. This is why the ego cannot take an action of any sort that we could call surrender or letting go or acceptance.

There are methods that say you can work with effort, super-effort, using your will, using very strong intention. This kind of work can activate some essential states, but at the expense of solidifying the core further. If you use effort in your work, if you use pushing, which is possible to some extent, you might have development, but you will be solidifying your defenses. And the most important thing that the solidification of the defenses does is that it closes the heart. It closes the tenderness, the vulnerability, the gentleness, the softness, the smoothness. You might have power, it's true, but you do not have the part that can enjoy.

All this means that we don't actually do anything in the process of understanding. What needs to happen is just an awareness of the fact that you're resisting, an understanding of the process of resistance. When you understand it, your interest in resistance stops. All you can do is allow that to happen; the rest is not up to you. The rest is up to Essence. That's why it is sometimes called grace. Grace can descend and dissolve you. It can make you part of it. But you cannot let go, you cannot surrender, you cannot accept. You can only see that you are rejecting, that you're not surrendering, that you're not letting go. Then you are seeing the activity of the ego.

When there is surrender and letting go, there is no activity and ego is not there. The cessation of resistance, the cessation of rejection, the cessation of defense, is also the dissolution of that part of the personality. It may bring fear because you believe that you will disappear. And you may be concerned about who will do what is required if you don't do it. You need trust and confidence in Essence here.

When you really see that the nature of the personality is reactivity, a cyclic reactivity, when you see the whole cycle of ego activity based on hope, desire and rejection, it is possible that the activity will cease, and peace and stillness will arise. Then it is possible to understand what Being is. When this happens, you'll discover that even if there is action and activity, where you come from is peace and stillness.

This peace and stillness that you are coming from is exactly what your ego resists most of all. In fact, the first experience of peace is what the ego is trying to cover up with its reactivity. It is a kind of death experience, because you experience nothing there, just complete, absolute silence and blackness. That is peace, complete peace. There is no action, no reaction, no nothing. Just complete silence, complete peace.

You might actually be engaged in some activity, but where you are coming from, your fundamental attitude, is that there is no reaction to anything, no rejection of anything. If you allow this to happen, then it is possible to know what Being is.

Essentially, this experience of peace, of death, is that you are not reacting, and that you *are not*. There is precisely the feeling of "I am not." I am not, and so there is no reactivity. The full experience of Being is a little beyond this, is more a feeling that "I am," but I am not reacting.

Ultimately, we are Being. The process of the Work includes the goal, because from the beginning, in the process of understanding yourself, the perspective is toward Being, not toward doing some activity. If you are reacting in the work on yourself, you are perpetuating the personality. But if you understand from the beginning that this reaction and activity of the personality is itself a non-Being, is a resistance against Being, then perhaps your orientation will be more influenced by Being. So the goal is in you from the beginning.

Now, Being is very mysterious. To truly understand the action of the personality, to understand that it is a cyclic movement of reactivity, you must know Being. It is the contrast with Being that reveals the core reactivity. That's why I have said that you need to go to the sharp edge between reactivity and Being, and when they are next to each other in your experience, you can say, "Yes, this is reaction."

Before you know Being, before you are Being, you are too identified with the personality to get a perspective on it. When you are Being, you are aware of its stillness and objectivity and can see in contrast the feverish activity of the contracted personality. You see that there's nothing intrinsically there. There's a contraction, there is movement, pushing and pulling, and there is frustration.

The complete perception of the hopelessness of the situation, the realization that your feverish attempts to alter yourself are futile, can bring about the cessation of the activity. The cessation is sometimes called death, which is peace. Then it is possible for us to know Being.

So what is Being? Being is alive and still at the same time. In Being, you know that you are alive, that you are, but there is no movement; there is just complete stillness. There is stillness through and through. Even though the deepest level of the body is full of movement—the blood circulation and movement within all the cells and even the movement of the atoms—Being is deeper than all of that. Being has no agitation whatsoever.

Being is new, always new, and the personality is old, because it is always generated from the past. Personality always feels somewhat stale compared to Being. It is a leftover. Personality is the remains of the past that have not been completely digested, metabolized and eliminated; it would have been eliminated long ago if it had been completely understood, and could therefore dissolve. Personality is always getting older, fermenting, while Being is always fresh, always new, it is nowness itself.

It is so difficult to say anything about Being; in a sense, all you can say is that you are. Being is a presence—when you are, you are present. It's the absence of reaction to anything inside or outside, past or future. People think that if they stop reacting there will be fear or suffering, but fear and suffering are still reactions. Personality is just projecting its experience onto Being, because it can't imagine anything else. If you experience fear or suffering, you haven't stopped reacting. If you think that you will be miserable or bored or scared if you cease reactivity, you don't understand what Being is. To the personality, Being is unknown.

S: You've often told us that everyone has experiences of essential states, but they don't recognize them. For me, the state of just Being is one of the hardest to grasp—it just comes and goes and bounces around in intermittent waves.

AH: Is Being coming and going or is the personality coming and going? When it goes, the experience of Being arises, so it might appear that the Being comes and goes. That is how most people experience Essence—that it comes and goes.

S: So what is the relationship between Being and external activity?

AH: That's the question of doing. We first need to be clear about what Being is. First of all, Being is a homogeneous presence. Being is not many parts relating to one another. In Being, there are no partitions—it is all one thing just like a pool of water is all water. It is not oil and water; there are no separations. You are this pool, and the boundaries of this pool don't exist; it goes forever. So there is unity and stillness, because nothing moves in it, yet there is a sense of existence and beingness.

Being is the nature of Essence. The main quality of Essence is that it is Being. The quality of Being, rather than any particular quality of Essence, is what makes Essence different from personality. Being is a unity with no partitions, no boundaries, no movement, no reaction, but a fullness, a plenitude through and through. This is our true nature, and it can be the source of everything in us, all our actions.

Now, the question arises, how do you take action? What is action, what is doing if I am not reacting? How do I do anything? How do I get up? How do I reach for my food, or touch someone? Do I have to do it again by contracting, by suffering and trying to get somewhere? Is there any way to do action without that cycle of frustration?

To understand what true action is, we need to recall what we know about the activity of personality. We have seen that the activity of the personality, what we usually call doing, is actually a contraction, a solidification of body and mind that brings the contractions together, makes them one-pointed in a sense. The one-pointedness is what we call the ego identity, and it seems to push in a certain way. We are operating from this tension and we call it our identity—"I am doing this."

So when you are taking action from this place you're actually saying no to Being, pushing against it. There is no way to truly act from the personality. We have seen that when we understand the activity of the personality—the contracting and pushing the body into action—it dissolves. If you are not engaged in this rejection of Being, Being is there. You are no longer identifying with the frustrated core which pushes away reality. So you can truly act when the identity is Being itself. You are Being. When you are the beingness it is possible to see what real action is.

The way the real action of Being works is similar to what happens in the personality action. We have seen that in the personality, the contraction solidifies or thickens to create support or will. This becomes a stepping stone for the action of personality. When there is action on the level of Being, Being attains a dynamic quality. There is actually a kind of condensation that becomes will. Being is then experienced as will. It attains a new quality, as if it moves or is being oriented; Being itself takes direction, alignment, and focus. But Being is One. So when Being acts, it is not aligned with something else but with itself, and it acts on all points at the same time. As in a pool of water, each drop, each atom is in concert. All of them move in one direction, toward one point. So there is no conflict, no tension between one and another.

When there is no split, no separation between what you take yourself to be and Being itself, then Being becomes lived; it is like the action of a tiger. What motivates a tiger? Where do the actions come from? Is there part of the tiger that wants to do something and another that doesn't want to do anything or wants to do something different? Is there a kind of meeting together of different motivations and then they do it? Does the tiger have inner conflicts? When the tiger jumps, is it ambivalent? Is part of it holding back? No. If the tiger jumps, everything jumps. It is a complete action —one-pointed, no boundaries, no mind. Just action. Being just acts. Being doesn't move, it's still. But it attains a state of true will in the sense that there is a focusing and orientation of Being. It is as if all the atoms in Being were aligned toward one magnetic pole, and it might feel like a growing force. In a magnet, all the atoms are aligned in the same direction, so the magnetic field increases, and that creates a force. The actual Being is like the magnet; in Being the atoms are aligned, and a force and a tremendous focus are created. You can experience Being as a force with a direction from everywhere; it has an energetic sense to it, a feeling of instinct, a feeling that the roots themselves are ready to act. Essentially you become like the tiger. The action is spontaneous, unified, complete, total, clear, specific, with no confusion and no mind.

S: Does Being have preference? Say, about whether we blow the world up or not?

AH: Being has no mind. When you are the Being, Being is not experienced as your own being. There is no American Being or Russian Being. There is no earth's Being separate from the sun's Being. There isn't this galaxy's Being and then the rest of the universe's Being. Being is One all the way through. The Being acts in unity in one action; and the action of Being, because it comes from Being, takes into consideration the whole of existence in an instant. So mind is not involved.

Such action is called instinctual because it acts the way it is supposed to act. When the tiger acts, it acts. It's not thinking of other tigers. It's not thinking about whether there will be war or peace. The action is complete, and it's the right action.

Such action is beyond mind. Even if there is preference, the preference itself is an action initiated by Being. When there is a need for action, Being responds, it does not react. Being responds by manifesting a state, a quality that is needed objectively at the moment.

To understand will in relation to Being is a very subtle thing. It's happening all the time. When you move your hand, it's the action of Being. If you bat your eyelashes, it's Being. The actions that we have no emotional conflicts with are done with great ease and fluidity by Being. Your mind does not need to be involved with them. We take these actions of Being for granted, and never notice that Being is acting. This acting of Being is also the expression of will.

Usually the action of the personality separates our mind from our Being, and then we want to figure out what to do and what not to do. So we are not allowing our Being to actually act. Yet it is acting all the time. The majority of our actions are done by Being. If you allow your identity to be the Being, you'll see that Being is not separate from the body, or even from the mind, instead it is the very nature of the body, the very nature of the mind, even the very nature of the personality. In Being there is no boundary and no separation. That means the action is coming from the ground, the source, Being, so it is real doing and involves all levels at once, from the bottom up. It's as if the Being radiates from the bottom of a lake and creates a wave that radiates throughout the whole thing. Everything is involved —mind, body, spirit, emotion—and is happening in one direction. And that direction, when Being is focused in one place, is what we call essential identity, the essential self.

The true identity arises when there is a need for an essential action. When there is no need for a response, there is no essential identity, there is just Being in repose: no activity, no mind, no body, no nothing, just stillness. When a tiger is not acting, just lying there, it doesn't know anything, it doesn't think of itself as tiger. It is just Being. When it acts, it becomes one-pointed, and that one-pointedness is at that moment the identity of the tiger.

True action is the boundless Being becoming one-pointed, and that will be a personal action. But that Being, that universal Being, is always acting everywhere. The creation of one point, which is your own action, which is your own self, is one of the manifestations of Being.

Everyone is in action in the Being all the time. That is why it is said that if you are willing to be aligned to the supreme will, there is no end to the plenitude that you can achieve in your life. This is because your action is the most correct action, the action that goes with all the rest of existence, and it can only benefit everything and everybody involved including you at all levels. It is the most unifying action.

It is hard to know the action of Being, if a person doesn't know Being, is not Being. We have only the personality action, which is reactivity, as a model. But when we know Being, it is possible to know doing. So, doing presupposes Being, and doing is like the action of a tiger.

S: And are you aware then that you are Being?

AH: Oh yes, you are aware that you are Being.

S: It's not the unconscious?

AH: No, it is not the unconscious—when you are Being, you are awake. You are acutely aware of everything; but the awareness is not self-reflective. It is like the eye when it is open—it sees other things, but it doesn't see itself. When you reflect back on yourself, you don't see anything, just Being.

Experiencing pure Being means, more than anything else, that you get out of the way; you cease. To cease means to stop reacting, which means you become aware that you were reacting. This awareness itself is the action of Being.

Then you are not doing according to your opinions or preferences, but you are surrendering to the supreme will. Most of the time, because we are identified with the personality, we are busy reacting and we complain that we are suffering. There is no possibility of ending the suffering unless you cease reacting and become Being. Suffering can't end because it is the very process of your reaction. You can dislike it, hate it, try to do something about it, try to run away from it, pretend that it's not true. But it is not going to change. The sooner you know that the suffering is the very process of your reaction, the sooner your suffering will cease. You might be reacting to what I'm saying. You might be saying, "I don't like this," and try to do something else, but whatever you do will lead you back to this same result. So the personality saying yes, means that the personality ceases, it gives up. Then there is Being, with all the possibilities of doing—effortless, spontaneous doing.

This effortless spontaneous doing is directly experienced as a flow, a current. The presence of Being is experienced as flowing with its own will and direction. The flow of Being, the continuity of Being, is the action, is the real doing. This can be experienced in many ways depending on the clarity and subtlety of one's perception. Being is experienced as dynamic, a dynamic stillness that is the source of all actions.

THIRTEEN

Humanness, Vulnerability and Being

S ince next week is Christmas, I thought we'd discuss something that's relevant to the season. We'll discuss what makes Christmas possible. In particular, I want to explore the statement that Christ made, "The meek shall inherit the earth." Is this statement true? Obviously, most people don't think so. It seems that the one who inherits the earth is the one who has more nuclear bombs. I'm not saying that I will explain exactly what Jesus meant. I will just say what I understand, what comes to my mind about what it might mean. I'm not really going to say anything new to you, just bring in some facts that you all know and pull them together. In this way we will be able to see an implication that we usually miss.

To understand the meaning of "the meek shall inherit the earth," we must understand what it means to be human.

Let's try to understand what it really means to be human, what characterizes a human, what it means to say, "I am human, I feel human." What I see is that to be really human is the thing that most humans don't want to be. To really allow oneself to be human in the genuine sense of the word seems to most people's minds to be very undesirable. One reason being human is seen to be so undesirable is that to most of us the word "meek" means something that is undesirable for living one's life.

Compared to other living beings on earth, we humans are, in a sense, much less fortunate; our very human nature brings us certain difficulties that other animals don't experience. For instance, compared to a human being, what an alligator experiences can be considered very fortunate. An alligator just lives, swims, walks, eats, and that's it. No problem. It dies and it is not even afraid of dying. I'm talking about an alligator instead of another animal because an alligator is a good contrast to the word "meek." An alligator doesn't go through what we have to go through.

It is very well known that we human beings are physically less adapted, weaker, more vulnerable to the environment than other creatures. We are meek in the sense that physically we're pretty much dependent on the environment. Especially when we're babies, we're completely, one-hundred-percent helpless. Most animals are not that helpless. Some come out of the womb and start walking immediately. They need only a short period of nurturing and caring, and then they can take care of themselves. Physical vulnerability is a fact about having a human body. We're physically dependent on our environment almost all of our lives and we cannot withstand much pressure from it.

We are vulnerable not only physically, but also mentally. We can be conscious of our situation—we can reflect on it, know its implications, and understand it. Our human mind is so impressionable, so influenceable, that the best word to describe it is vulnerable. The fact that it is so influenceable, susceptible, and impressionable leaves us open and vulnerable to absolutely everything. As a baby you are completely at the mercy of the environment not only physically but mentally. You are vulnerable in a way that influences you for the rest of your life. You're so susceptible to your parents and the rest of your environment that almost everything about how you feel and how you think is determined from outside: what you think is good, what you think is bad, what you think you want, what you think you don't want, even who you think you are. Animals cannot really be conditioned in that way, because their minds are not that impressionable.

Not only are we very vulnerable physically and mentally, but we're emotionally vulnerable as well. Some animals are somewhat vulnerable emotionally, but we human beings are completely vulnerable emotionally. We are probably the most emotionally vulnerable creatures on earth. Our capacity to feel makes us emotionally vulnerable, puts us in a very vulnerable position. Emotionally we're susceptible to the experience of whatever state is happening in our bodies. We can experience pleasure and experience pain. We feel love, but also hatred. Our vulnerability is a total openness to any possibility.

If you let yourself be really human and not cover up your vulnerability, you'll see that you're completely under the influence of reality. If you let yourself be, you can experience intense love, intense pain, or tremendous fear. You not only can experience tremendous fear, but can actually know that you are feeling afraid, and that you will actually die. Animals might be in certain states, but they don't really feel them in the way that we do.

Our vulnerability is not the only characteristic of being human, but it is a uniquely human characteristic. It means that we're influenceable, impressionable, and open. Many other creatures are by their very constitutions defended. That's why I mentioned an alligator. An alligator doesn't feel emotional hurt, right? It doesn't feel that it loves someone, then gets rejected and feels hurt and abandoned. As far as we know, by its very nature, it's defended, because it doesn't have the capacity to feel. Through our capacity to think and to know, to know our nature and our destiny, we're vulnerable to all kinds of feelings—fears, conflicts, and the like.

If you see this situation clearly, you'll observe that you're actually terrified of this vulnerability, and that in most circumstances you avoid it. You probably see it as meekness, weakness, dependence. But however you see it, it remains the most uniquely human characteristic.

So far we have discussed vulnerability from the perspective of our usual view of it, which we see as a weakness, a meekness, an undefendedness. To be vulnerable means to be defenseless, at the mercy of what you feel. And, as you know, most of what you feel is at the mercy of your environment.

This is how we are born—completely vulnerable—and that characteristic never goes away. However, we deal with the vulnerability by desensitizing ourselves. We make ourselves thick-skinned, like alligators. And we end up believing that to be able to live on this earth among other humans, we have to be like alligators or turtles, depending on how aggressive or passive we are.

And if you observe most people, you will see that they are rather like alligators or turtles, in the sense that they walk around inside thick shells to protect themselves, to hide, to cover up their basic vulnerability. This is because we experienced as children, and we still experience, that we can be completely flooded by feelings. When you're sad, your sadness can feel miles deep, and when you're angry, you can feel like a ball of fire, and when you're hurt, you can feel completely devastated, and when you're jealous, you're burning with suffering. Our capacity to feel is tremendous. The basic reaction to it at a deep level is to feel that it's too much: "I don't know whether I can handle this. I'm at the mercy of these storms." So we slowly and diligently build thick shells to protect ourselves and, we believe, to survive.

Believing that we need to be thick-skinned to survive is not something we hide from ourselves; it's completely accepted in our society. We are told that to get ahead, we have to become more thick-skinned and not feel things. And this point of view is actually rationalized with all kinds of philosophies.

But something happens when we build a shell and hide inside it, which is the source of most human complaints. When we cover up our vulnerability so that we're not open to hurt and pain, fear and influenceability, we also become insensitive to joy, love, happiness, pleasure, and aliveness.

This helps us understand further what vulnerability means. It is true that we are physically vulnerable, but if you look at the physical vulnerability of a human being, you see that that vulnerability itself is also an asset. This vulnerability gives us the capacity to adapt better than other creatures. Vulnerability ultimately means sensitivity, transparency, penetrability. We see it as influenceability, which we think is negative, but it actually means that we're open, we can be penetrated, we're sensitive to impressions coming into us and going out of us. This leaves us at the mercy of all kinds of influences, but also gives us the possibility of greater versatility and flexibility in terms of what we can do, how we can respond, what environments we can live in. We can adapt and respond differently to different stimuli. Human beings have been able to adapt to and live in all kinds of environments. Most other creatures can't do that because they have a narrower range of responses. We have been able to adapt because of our mental, emotional, and physical vulnerability.

Another element of our vulnerability which can be seen as a mixed blessing is knowing we are vulnerable, and being able to conceive of the implications of that vulnerability. This leaves us in a very precarious position: We know we can die and we know what kinds of things can kill us. We know we can be hurt and we know what kinds of things can hurt us. For example, just the fact that we know of the existence of nuclear energy leaves us vulnerable. Animals don't even know there is such a thing and they don't fear being destroyed because they don't have that vulnerability. We have it. But that vulnerability also gives us a certain ability to work with the environment. Animals cannot do anything about the things that threaten them which they don't know about, while we can deal with these same threats because we know about them. And we know about them because of our vulnerability.

So we can see how the human element is a mixed blessing. It's a vulnerability, but in a sense it's also a strength. It gives us the capacity and flexibility to deal with the environment. We have a greater range of responses, possibilities, feelings, and experiences than other creatures. Human beings are so vulnerable that they can be psychic. They can know there is an approaching danger without having to even know it consciously. Animals have this capacity to some extent, but only in terms of the immediate environment. Vulnerability here means sensitivity, as well as permeability.

As far as I can tell, we are the only beings who are permeable to everything that exists, from the most painful to the most sublime. We're sensitive not only to experiencing the pleasures and pains of our bodies, to feeling our emotions, the painful and the pleasurable, and to sensing our thoughts, but our vulnerability also gives us the possibility of experiencing, being aware of, being in contact with all levels of reality. We're permeable to not only physical, emotional, and mental stimuli, but to essential and spiritual stimuli as well. So, not only are we vulnerable in the sense that our feelings, our preferences, even our identity can be influenced, but we are also vulnerable to being aware, conscious, and permeable to our true identity, and to the nature of all existence.

So you see, our uniquely human quality of vulnerability is a disadvantage from one perspective, and a great advantage from another. We are wide open to all influences, all possibilities if we allow ourselves to be—if we don't defend ourselves, if we don't build a shell and hide behind it. Our human consciousness is so vulnerable that we can actually know who we are. We're so conscious, so permeable, that we can experience the very nature of all of reality—the nature of a stone, a tree, the nature of ourselves.

I will say more about what permeability means.

Permeability gives us the capacity to embody and express our nature in a way that is not possible for other creatures. A human being can be full of love and compassion and radiant with joy. Animals can't experience that. You don't see an animal radiant with joy. They're not permeable to such feelings, although to some extent they can perceive them. They can't experience them consciously, and they also can't express them. When a human being is loving, you can look at his or her face and see it. You can see that a human being is sad, a human being is happy, a human being is angry. And the deeper aspects of reality can only be expressed by humans. When I look at a human being, I can see him or her as truth. Can you look at a squirrel and see the squirrel expressing truth? You can't. A squirrel can't do that. It's too thick-skinned. It's not vulnerable to deeper reality.

We're aware of our vulnerability from very early on, and because the environment is difficult a lot of the time, we try to control it. One way we try to control it is by trying to feel only what is good and not what is painful; to feel the pleasure and happiness, and to avoid what is painful and unhappy. But that means we have to reduce our vulnerability. How can that happen? It's the same vulnerability which is permeable to both pleasure and pain.

An extreme attempt to eliminate our vulnerability is to try to not be permeable to anything—to not feel anything, the pain or the pleasure. And when you eliminate that vulnerability completely, when you don't feel anger or sadness, love or hate, need or desire, when you don't feel any emotion at all, you start feeling alienated and that you're not human. The effect is that you feel you're not human, because you've cut away the most characteristic of human qualities, your vulnerability. If you're completely invulnerable, completely defended with nothing flowing in or out, completely unfeeling, you're completely a shell. You feel, "I'm not human, I'm like a machine." It's true that you're defended then, but you're defended against all possibilities, not just against some.

So my understanding is that being meek means being vulnerable. The meek are vulnerable. The meek are the truly human. People think of meek as weak, but we have seen here that what meek really means is being permeable, vulnerable, feeling, knowing, sensing, being truly human. You're so vulnerable that not only can you block your vulnerability and eliminate your very human nature, but that same human vulnerability allows you to experience things that are more than human, beyond the human. This human vulnerability makes you permeable to the deepest nature of reality, to what is divine.

And if you look at what we do most of the time about this vulnerability, this characteristically human quality, you'll see that we're constantly saying "no" to it. We're constantly saying, "No, I don't want to be like that. I don't want to be that open, I don't want to be that vulnerable—it's scary, it's dangerous, it's threatening. I might be hurt, I might die, I might lose who I am." One of the greatest fears about vulnerability is that if I'm vulnerable, I'm going to lose my sense of who I am. I'll be so open to being influenced that I won't know who I am. I'll lose myself in the other person, or in nature, or in whatever. This is because vulnerability involves the awareness of no separation, the awareness of oneness.

What is oneness? Oneness is the supreme reality, the most fundamental characteristic of all reality. The ultimate truth of all reality is that it is one—one beingness. Without our vulnerability, we could not be aware of this. We cannot experience oneness if we are not vulnerable. And this is the larger implication of being vulnerable. Since vulnerability means permeability to the awareness of oneness, ultimately vulnerability means you're not separate.

When you are aware of oneness, when you see that you and everyone else and everything else are completely one, vulnerability will not be seen as a disadvantage at all. The moment your vulnerability is complete and you are aware of oneness, there is no fear. When you are completely vulnerable, completely not separating yourself from anyone or anything, when you know that you are the oneness, that your very nature is the unity, is the supreme reality, then you know that in your deepest, most intimate, absolute nature and identity you can't die—nothing can happen to you. You're one-hundred-percent invulnerable.

Complete, one-hundred-percent, absolute and total vulnerability is the same thing as complete, one-hundred-percent, absolute and total invulnerability. In fact, in our attempts to eliminate our vulnerability, to deaden ourselves, desensitize ourselves, create a shell around ourselves, we create fear. The shell is always scared, as well as isolated. Separate from the world. There's no unity, no support from the universe. You are on your own. You are cut off. And when you are cut off, you're vulnerable. Then vulnerability is seen as dangerous.

Vulnerability is a danger only if you think of yourself as separate from the rest of existence. This means that vulnerability is seen as a danger only if it is not completely understood.

Vulnerability is a danger only if you think that there is a me and there is an other, and that I'm not defended against that other. This experience of vulnerability is not complete. There is still a barrier. You're only partially permeable. You still have a shell, and the shell lets some things in and out, but not everything.

When the shell becomes completely permeable, completely transparent, completely vulnerable, when there is no shell anymore, just empty space, then the question arises: Who's there to be scared of what? What does it mean to be scared? What does it mean to be vulnerable? We protect ourselves because we believe we are vulnerable. But by that very protection we change vulnerability from being the greatest support to being the greatest danger. If you're not vulnerable, you're separate. If you're separate, you're scared. You're scared of everything.

The complete understanding of vulnerability is that the nature of the human being is ultimately the supreme reality, is this unity, is everything. The human is the possibility of being the supreme reality. We are the final, ultimate fruit of existence, because we are the most vulnerable. Creation evolves from the least vulnerable to the most vulnerable. Rocks are less vulnerable than trees, and trees are less vulnerable than animals, and animals are less vulnerable than humans.

Reality has to become completely vulnerable, all the way to the utmost possibility of vulnerability. And when that happens at the very tip of development, at the ultimate apogee of evolution, you experience yourself at the utmost vulnerability, and you see you are everything, you are the nature of everything. So, if you go through total meekness, total weakness, total susceptibility and total vulnerability, leaving yourself at the mercy of everything, and if you allow yourself to be completely, totally at the mercy of reality, you realize you *are* the reality.

The fact and the awareness of our vulnerability are part of what pushes us to realize that we are the reality. Because we are aware of our vulnerabilities, we don't rest; we want to find complete security. We want to feel that we're not vulnerable. We want complete invulnerability. And if you really look and find complete invulnerability, it is the supreme reality.

You can find the supreme reality only through your human nature; you cannot find it through resisting your human nature. If you resist the vulnerability of your human nature, you'll go backward in your evolution, becoming more like a rock or a crocodile. If you allow yourself to become vulnerable to your vulnerability, if you become more human, more transparent, more permeable, then you move forward in your humanity and become more human. And as we've seen, only the human being can move to the state of unity, because only the human can be completely vulnerable.

We've seen that vulnerability allows us to be influenced, to be penetrated, to be affected. And usually we see this as bad, because we believe that many influences are dangerous or hostile to us. So we reduce our receptivity. If, however, we allow ourselves to be influenceable, which means to allow our vulnerability, then we will discover that what we are primarily influenced by is our own deeper inner nature.

This tells us something about the personality. The personality tries not to be influenceable. It wants to be the influencer, the actor, the doer, the one who's in control, the one who directs. It wants to do that even in relationship to our Essence. The personality wants to experience Essence, but it also wants to still be in charge. It tries to do this by eliminating its vulnerability, by saying no to it just like it does to everything else. It makes itself opaque. But if the personality understands what vulnerability actually means, then we become receptive to our deeper nature, and it acts on us. We are no longer the actor; we are a permeable membrane. We are acted upon, we are penetrated by our nature, and we allow it to come out. And the work on the personality, which can be seen as refining it, allows that membrane to become increasingly vulnerable to our Essence. The less defended and opaque the personality is, the more it is permeable to Essence. And as Essence manifests through the personality—as it permeates it, as it influences it, as the personality becomes completely one-hundred-percent vulnerable to our truest nature—we begin to see that there is no difference between them. We experience oneness, unity.

So, the meek shall inherit the earth. The vulnerable can experience the totality of all the possibilities on earth, at all levels. In fact, the meek will not only inherit the earth, they will inherit everything.

Vulnerability is needed for awareness and objectivity, for objective consciousness. This is because objective consciousness means awareness and understanding of exactly what is there. You can't understand exactly what is there if you don't want to be vulnerable. Understanding and vulnerability go together.

For instance, when I started talking to you today, I thought it would be a good idea to talk about the characteristically human quality of vulnerability. I had some things in mind to say, but I was also vulnerable to knowing that I didn't understand everything about it. So how am I going to gain understanding? Obviously the way to do it is by letting myself be vulnerable to the perceptions that arise, to let myself be acted upon. And that's where my understanding comes from. I learn from these talks just as you learn. I allow myself to be vulnerable, to be influenced by the source of understanding by letting myself from the beginning see what I know and what I don't know, by not blocking the perception that I don't know. I allow the possibility that there is more that I can know and that I don't even know how I will know it. When I am vulnerable in that way, what is needed will come. So really, every time I sit here and talk with you, I am allowing myself to be vulnerable. I can do this because my personality is a very permeable membrane. In other words, I can talk to you like this by allowing myself to be human, and so I can be permeable about whatever it is I'm talking about. I'm not a special case; any human being has this capacity. If you don't go against the movement of evolution, if you don't say no to your humanity, you'll be equally permeable, impressionable, influenceable by reality.

To be human means that you don't say, "I want this to happen," or "I don't want that to happen." You're so vulnerable that you don't need to choose what you experience. Whatever comes, comes. There's no resistance to it. When I say that to be human you don't choose this over that, I don't mean that if you feel yourself choosing, you should tell yourself not to choose, because then you're choosing. To be human is to be completely spontaneous, so delicate that you can't resist or say no to any experience.

Then you become like water—light goes through you. To be human is to be like delicate water, very clean, very transparent, very fresh. It doesn't have any opaqueness; it is completely colorless. You can see all colors through it. It's very fluid, transparent. Whatever impression comes from within you goes through you like light through water. To be vulnerable is to flow like water. To be like a running stream with the freshness of running water. There is a clarity, a lucidity, a delicacy. Vulnerability is like water, but the water is very delicate. It's like the water of tears—so delicate, so fine. If you are like tears, if your very nature is like colorless tears, then you feel what it's like to be vulnerable.

You see, we are afraid. We believe we need to separate ourselves, create thick shells and defend ourselves against impressions of all kinds, because we feel separate from the invulnerable reality, the state of unity. And we separate ourselves from the invulnerable reality by trying not to be vulnerable. By trying not to be vulnerable, we become vulnerable in a negative way. We believe that complete invulnerability would mean complete defensiveness, complete isolation and detachment from all experience. We don't see objectively what vulnerability is; we don't see that complete invulnerability means complete openness. Complete openness means the lack of all separateness. The absence of all boundaries means unity, which means invulnerability.

However, we go at it the other way around. We try to find invulnerability by isolating and defending ourselves, by becoming less sensitive, less human. But when we attempt to resist the vulnerability, when we say the slightest no to vulnerability, we're creating a boundary, a shell which makes us feel separate. And that very separateness makes us vulnerable to fears, makes us paranoid. There is no paranoia if there is unity.

Any questions?

Student: Do the misfits of our society develop by becoming so invulnerable that they go backwards to the animal state? They can't adapt and they become criminal?

A.H. Almaas: People who can't adapt are usually people who are blocking their vulnerability. As we've seen, vulnerability is on the surface an adaptation. Criminals might appear to be vulnerable to society's laws and to the police, but they are not vulnerable to their own feelings, to their own nature. They are, in fact, trying to protect themselves. The anger and the hatred that they express is an attempt to create a shell against their vulnerability. And because they're not vulnerable, they're not objective about their situation and they don't know what is dangerous and what is not dangerous.

If you're defended, your vulnerability is somewhat opaque. You don't allow all the influences to affect you, so you are only selectively aware of your environment, and can't be objective about the situation. If you are vulnerable, you can be aware of the whole situation because your vulnerability allows whatever is there to come in to you.

S: I've heard you talk about vulnerability in terms of love, like a completely loving state. Could you say some more about that?

AH: We're vulnerable because we feel, and more than anything, we try to cut off the depth of our capacity to feel. Now, complete openness to feeling means openness to love, because ultimately feeling is love. The origin of all feeling is love. The first feeling is love. If you follow your feelings all the way back, what will you come to finally? You can go on and on through many feelings, and eventually you find that the basic feeling is love.

You're most vulnerable when you're experiencing love. Beyond love is unity, where vulnerability and invulnerability become one. Love is the first emanation, the first particularization of the supreme reality, which is unity. The first expression, the first breath of the unity is divine universal love, with its sweetness and delicacy. That is where you are the most vulnerable, before your vulnerability becomes invulnerability. When you're loving, you still feel at the mercy of everything. The step beyond that is to become even more vulnerable, and then you're completely invulnerable. So we're seeing how love can lead all the way to complete vulnerability and thus to invulnerability.

Love is the highest, the deepest, the most intense, the most expansive possibility of feeling. Love is the heart. Beyond love is the supreme reality, which is beyond feeling or no feeling.

So vulnerability is vulnerability to love, and extremely deep vulnerability is love. If you really are vulnerable, you're loving. You can't help but be loving. And if you're very loving, you can't help but feel vulnerable. If you allow yourself to feel, your heart is completely open.

The love which is the first emanation from the supreme reality is Christ love, or boundless love. It is like a boundless heart, a heart with no barriers, no boundaries, no defenses. Heart with no boundaries at all *is* boundless love. There are no boundaries at all, no barriers at all, no defenses at all. So you are completely vulnerable. This is why love, completely divine, universal Christ love brings the greatest vulnerability: when you experience it, you are at the maximum of vulnerability before you feel yourself as invulnerable. You have to open yourself to that level before you can be invulnerable. And you can't do it by saying, "I'm doing this so I will become invulnerable." That very thought is a barrier. You have to be vulnerable with no defenses, without even the thought of a defense.

One way I see our situation is that creation or the universe is like a tree. Love is the flowers of the tree, and the human being is the final fruit of the tree, the final fruit of creation. The thick nectar of the ripe fruit is gratitude. Gratitude for how things are, gratitude for being vulnerable, gratitude that you can be completely influenceable. Gratitude for being human.

S: I'm sitting here trying to be permeable and vulnerable, and my body shuts down and I'm fighting sleep.

AH: You can't try to be vulnerable. That's the thing about vulnerability. When you try, you're already saying no to something. You want to change one thing to another. And by saying no to something, you're not letting yourself be vulnerable.

S: And that's what creates the resistance?

AH: Yes, ultimately resistance is trying to change things.

S: Maybe I should be vulnerable to the resistance.

AH: Right! That's how you start.

S: But then I go to sleep.

AH: If you're really vulnerable to the resistance, you're aware of the resistance. Going to sleep means not being vulnerable to the awareness of the resistance. The more you understand, the more you become vulnerable. You can't try to be vulnerable. Vulnerability means not choosing, remember? Resistance by its very nature is to say, "This, not that." If you say, "I don't want the resistance," you're adding another resistance. To be vulnerable means not to act, but rather to be acted upon.

S: You mean, you have to be present to be vulnerable.

AH: Yes, but if you try to be present, you're not being vulnerable. How to get there is all of our Work. Understanding and awareness are needed. You have to see how you're resisting, and how ultimately you're resisting vulnerability. To see this requires very deep, subtle understanding. And, as I've said, you can't be vulnerable by trying to be. In listening to these talks, the best thing is to not try to do anything; just listen and don't do anything else. Don't try to act on yourself, just be ears. Your hearing is your most susceptible sense. And what comes through your ears may act on you. The only thing the personality can do is to let or not let in influence.

S: So you don't even try to be present then.

AH: Ultimately, no. I don't try to be present.

S: It just happens.

AH: For a long time you have to try to be present, because the tendency is to not be present. You have to use your will to counteract that tendency. But there comes a time when trying to be present becomes a barrier, because it has to happen naturally. And at that point, the more you try to be present, the more you separate yourself from your presence. Because presence itself doesn't try to be present. So for a while, yes, you try, because your unconscious tendency is to not be present. You counteract that tendency with all kinds of measures until a time comes when you can will yourself to be present.

Then the next step is to see how you can be present without using your will, to let go of your attempt, your trying and have your presence still be there. Understanding is what's needed here. You need to see that the attempt to be present has nothing to do with being vulnerable. Trying is using forceful, active will which is the opposite of vulnerability. That's why methods that are oriented towards just developing will—trying and super-efforts and so on—block vulnerability. You can only go some of the way using those methods. But then you need to let go of that effort and allow vulnerability, allow the heart to open, and then you can be present without effort.

So there is a place for trying to be present. But in time, the more you become present, you see that there is tension; there is a me trying to do something and there is the presence. You see that actually the presence doesn't want anything, doesn't try anything. You start wondering: What's this? How can I try to be present? Who is trying to be present? And that's when you allow yourself to be influenced and affected by presence. That's when you learn to be vulnerable.

Vulnerability has its own emotional issues. People block vulnerability because of various emotional traumas from childhood. Understanding these traumas will allow the possibility of vulnerability. This is one reason we work on emotional understanding. The more you understand your emotions and why you block them, the more you allow yourself to be vulnerable.

S: It seems that certain spiritual systems have developed techniques to block vulnerability at certain levels. For example, mantras seem to be devoted to blocking vulnerability to mental activity. And maybe there are others. My question is about the usefulness of these techniques.

AH: That is not true. Some mantras are developed to allow vulnerability, to open the heart and relax the mind. Mantras can be used to block vulnerability, but I think that the original use for them is to allow vulnerability.

Any technique can be used to increase vulnerability. Even the technique of using the will can be used on the side of vulnerability, if there is a complete understanding of what will is.

S: I was also thinking that physical systems in spiritual techniques like sitting in a certain position seem to block being vulnerable to your body, being spontaneous to your body.

AH: They may block vulnerability, but it's possible that the people who originated these practices understood this. Like will, you can use them at the beginning to block your vulnerability, but if you understand this, you will see that at some point you have to change your course. A good technique shows you at some point that it has to be let go of; a good technique by its very nature exposes itself as a barrier at some point.

Vulnerability means not doing anything, so ultimately, vulnerability brings you to a point of not using any technique. Using any technique means you're choosing one thing over another, and vulnerability means exactly the absence of choosing. It means you're allowing yourself to be open.

So for instance, in this work we develop the ability to be more present in the body, and to allow certain essential qualities to arise in us. At a certain point you might feel, I can sense, look, and listen, I can be in my Hara, I can understand things, I can allow my will to come through, I can make things change, and so on. But you know that these capacities are still not enough. You must then let go of all the powers, all the capacities and not do anything, just let yourself be vulnerable, completely at the mercy of all forces.

This doesn't mean that you should go lie down in the street and say, "I'm going to let myself be vulnerable." That's not vulnerability; that's being thick-skinned, and not being vulnerable to your intelligence. To be vulnerable is,

as I have said, to allow yourself to be vulnerable to awareness, to objectivity, to understanding.

S: So you don't make choices if you're completely vulnerable?

AH: No, if you're completely vulnerable, you don't make
choices. In a sense, choices are made for you. Your inner
source moves in a certain direction. You become like a glove,
and Essence is the hand that moves you. The glove doesn't
make a choice. If the glove makes a choice, it won't let the
hand move. If the glove says, "No, I want to go this way,"
and the hand says, "No, I want to go that way," you're in
conflict. That's what emotional conflict is all about. But if
you don't choose and you let Essence, your nature, function
through you, the glove will be permeable, vulnerable to the
hand, and then your nature will move you. And your nature
has intelligence.

We don't trust that our nature has intelligence, that it will
know where to go, what to do. So, we don't let ourselves
be vulnerable to it. We feel we have to choose. But when we
are truly vulnerable, the choice is always to go along with the
supreme will. We don't go against it, ever. Our choice is to
be vulnerable to the supreme will, which is our true nature.

S: In a sense, the choice is already made for us.

AH: It is you. The supreme nature is you, ultimately. The
glove is not you. We think we are the glove, while actually
we are the hand. We identify with the glove and say, "I want
to have my own will, my own choices." At some point we
realize we are not the glove, we're the hand. Then the best
thing for the glove is to not create any resistance to the hand,
to allow the hand to move the way it wants to. And the best
glove is one that moves, that is flexible and responsive.
Beyond that there's no duality. The glove becomes part of
the hand. It becomes like the skin of the hand.

The Diamond Approach^{SM} described in this book is taught in group and private settings in California and Colorado, by teachers certified by the Ridhwan Foundation.

For information, write:

> Ridhwan
> P.O. Box 10114
> Berkeley, California 94709-5114

> Ridhwan School
> P.O. Box 18166
> Boulder, Colorado 80308–8166

Satellite groups operate in other national and international locations. For information about these groups, or to explore starting a group in your area, taught by certified Ridhwan teachers, write:

> Ridhwan
> P.O. Box 10114
> Berkeley, California 94709-5114